Special Times

SPECIAL
Times

*Primary
School
Assemblies*

*Hundreds of
Reflections,
Suggestions
and Practical Ideas*

MICHAEL DEW

© Michael Dew 1997

The right of Michael Dew[author] to be identified as author[s] of this work has been asserted by [him/her/them] in accordance with the Copyright, Design and Patents Act 1988.

British Library Cataloguing in Publication Data. A catalogue record for this book is available from the British Library.

Published by Eagle, an imprint of Inter Publishing Service (IPS) Ltd, St Nicholas House, 14 The Mount, Guildford, Surrey GU2 5HN.

All rights reserved. No part of this publication may be reproduced or transmitted in any form or by any means, electronic or mechanical, including photocopying, recording or any information storage and retrieval system, without either prior permission in writing from the publisher or a licence permitting restricted copying. In the United Kingdom such licences are issued by the Publishers Licensing Society Ltd, 90 Tottenham Court Road, London W1P 9HE.

Cover by Dew Design. All photographs © Tear Fund and used with kind permission.
Typeset by Eagle Publishing
Printed by Bell & Bain, Glasgow
ISBN No: 0 86347 222 2

To all the staff and children, past and present, at Broomgrove Junior School, where a true spirit of co-operation helped us all to learn together.

CONTENTS

	Introduction	9
1	What's Ahead	14
2	Questioning Times	15
3	A Poem or Story	17
4	Look, Listen and . . . ?	20
5	Short Talks	23
6	Class-led Assemblies	28
7	Visitors	30
8	Links With The Wider Community	31
9	Learning New Songs	32
10	Retelling Bible Stories	34
11	Showing and Sharing	36
12	An Experience Recounted	38
13	Someone's Life Story	39
14	Using Puppets	40
15	Further Suggestions (including prayer)	42
16	Provocative Pictures	45
17	Introducing the Worked Examples of Assemblies	47
	1. The Wonder of Colour	50
	2. Co-operation	52
	3. Getting Along Together	54
	4. Lost and Found	56
	5. We All Have Feelings – Anger	58
	6. Channels	60
	7. Darkness and Light	62
	8. Creation	64
	9. Measurement	66
	10. People are People	68
	11. Ironmongery Inspirations	70
	12. 'Practice Makes Perfect'	72
	13. Fantasy and Imagination	74
	14. Obsessions	76
	15. The Rainbow	78
	16. Big and Small	80
	17. Personalities are Different	82
	18. Promises, Promises	84
18	Postscript	86

Appendices:

A	A Brief Recommended Booklist	87
B	Songbooks and Other Resources	89
C	Some Children's Answers	90
D	Conflict Resolution Rap and 'About Me'	92
E	Music . . . 'And God said'	94
F	Overhead Transparencies	95

INTRODUCTION

Putting the book and myself into context

After 20 years of Headship in two different schools I retired early in search of new opportunities. These have provided numerous links with well over a hundred schools to date. Discussions with teachers indicated that there was still a need for useable primary level 'Assembly' material. So this is my attempt to rake through the notes of hundreds of assemblies and help us both in the process. Where necessary, ideas have been altered or updated.

I use the word assembly advisedly – not solely out of nostalgia, but also from conviction. It is a word that reminds us that we are all gathering together for a specific purpose. To me, that purpose was to reinforce the oneness of the school as a family, a group of people working together, not classes and teachers in isolation. There, I have used twice already one of my favourite theme words – *together*. We always found the children quick to point these words out!

The threads woven into this overriding purpose include learning new songs, news, notices and sharing. Some would disagree, but I see no conflict between these functions and that of 'collective worship' as it has now become known. Indeed they can easily cross-fertilise and influence one another for good, with sensitive handling. Worship cannot be separated from life and is therefore an integral part of the assembly.

So, I believe that assembly is for the whole school, or large sections of the school, i.e. Juniors and Infants. Class worship may well have a place but it is no substitute for the gathering of the whole community. On the plus side, some variety in venue/size of group may well be conducive to different experiences. For example class worship may be a better opportunity for some individuals to state an opinion/feeling openly, than in a group of hundreds.

Many schools/governors/teachers are concerned that they may not be meeting the requirements of the law, which is often confusing in itself. The 1988 Education Act began the recent 're-thinking' by telling each school to 'provide a daily act of collective worship', which has to be inclusive and of high quality (amongst other things). Subsequent official attempts to specify the required content of such worship seem to me to have done little to clarify the already muddied waters. In a cosmopolitan society, the challenge has always been there. At the start of my second Headship I recall discussing with teachers, formally and informally, the content of our assemblies. Back in the 1970s, we had to realise that hymns and prayers, both lifted out of books, were not in themselves 'worship'. Teachers, quite rightly, who said they were atheist or agnostic, declared a feeling of hypocrisy and unease. Our solution at the time was to coin our own phraseology, so that we could all meet in an honest way.

I seem to remember saying things like 'OK, I understand your position. Feel free, just bring us something to reflect upon, a thought for the day. We do not have to always have a hymn and I would like us all to take part.'

The other side of the coin now, of course, is the legal demand upon us to provide worship in assembly which is 'wholly or mainly of a broadly Christian character'. Here I must declare my own position. As a practising, convinced Christian, I was quite happy to help to provide this element of the daily assemblies. Over the years my approach may have changed, my styles of delivery become more varied, but in essence I was delighted to have opportunities to share my faith, open up questions and read Bible stories, as appropriate. As a staff, we all knew that we could not make children or each other 'worship', but we could give each other meaningful and challenging thoughts or experiences. So that is what we set out to do. I thought then that we were meeting our legal requirements under the 1944 Education Act and we still are now, under that of 1988.

Therefore, I would urge all teachers to be open and honest with each other and the children, first and foremost. At the very least we can recognise and celebrate our common humanity. We can ask questions as a collective activity, without criticising or evaluating answers but accepting all offers of help. We can try to bring each other face to face with our feelings and worries, in a supportive way.

In assembly, as part of worship, we did over the years bring a wide variety of themes to the children. In them, we provided what we considered to be helpful experiences that perhaps –

1. Gave a focus or stillness for a while
2. Brought hope or humour
3. Stimulated to thought or action
4. Made us confront our own weaknesses
5. Developed a sense of wonder
6. Enabled us to share experiences
7. Celebrated achievements

This was never intended to be a fully inclusive list, simply guidelines so that all teachers and children could participate wholeheartedly.

It was after one of several conversations with Jehovah Witness parents, who thought perhaps their children should not be in assembly, that I decided to test my bold statement to them – 'Most of our assemblies you would find acceptable, we do not ram mainstream Christianity down the children's throats. We ask the children to be honest and think for themselves.' As in many frank discussions we found shared convictions, for example on the lack of evidence to support the theory of evolution (from one species to another) that led us to believe in a great God who created the world in six days.

They knew I was an active member of an evangelical church, of course, and our views of Jesus, for instance, were a source of disagreement. But for both of us this situation was different, we were talking about a state school. So I felt obliged to test the realities myself. Thereafter, not always very fully in the hurly-burly of daily school life, I kept a note of the content of our assemblies over nearly 14 years. They, and most parents, were satisfied, it would seem. For many years Muslims too were happily accommodated in our assemblies. It requires patience on both sides, taking time to listen and find common ground.

Differences between people and faiths are real, and have to be faced with tolerance. To my mind that is quite satisfactory, as long as the necessary subsequent action is agreed. Some parents did request their children to miss some assemblies, when content was known in advance, for instance. On the other hand, I never did try to explain another faith or religion in detail to the children although the main religions were referred to. To do this objectively is difficult and inviting a parent or religious leader to share the faith she/he holds is usually better. If considered desirable, a school *may* hold acts of worship broadly in the tradition of another religion and those which contain elements drawn from a number of faiths, but it is not obligatory. Learning about other faiths is now part of the RE National Curriculum, of course, but we are concerned here with collective worship, which, quite rightly, 'must be wholly or mainly of a broadly Christian character.'

Most local Standing Advisory Councils for Religious Education (SACRES) seem to take the

Introduction

same line. Back in the 1970s we too wanted to develop community spirit, relate assembly to the day to day life and concerns of the school, give children freedom to explore and express their views, encourage the asking of questions, and value imagination and contemplation in our zest for life. The aim remains pretty constant.

The format of this book is an attempt to summarise years of assemblies, reporting and then analysing and advising as we proceed. It is reminiscing with a view to passing on my experiences, and possibly wisdom! Many of the ideas are deliberately briefly presented so there is not too much to take in. Anyway, each of us has to develop an embryo of an idea and to make it our own. Any lack of interest and conviction will soon be detected by the children, and the moment is lost. Your own sincerity and enthusiasm is at the basis of a good presentation. I would encourage you to think well ahead and ruminate on your subject for a while. Adapt ideas to suit your situation, beforehand and during the assembly. Watch the children's faces!

I was at a barbecue recently, and as often happens, found myself talking with a total stranger who turned out to be a teacher! He told me that he loved taking assembly because of the lively reaction of the children. How wonderful, I thought, and asked, 'How do you maintain this rapport?' 'Eyeball to eyeball contact' was his reply . . . He is absolutely right.

So, it is your turn to take assembly . . . your concern to use the time well is excellent.

First stop and think . . . have I an experience, a story, a poem, an event in local or national news or a snippet of school life, that has recently affected me and that I can use as a beginning?

Ask yourself ... what has been covered recently in our assemblies, what left out (perhaps on an already agreed theme?). What is needed next to take the school on?

This is the way I worked. With everything else that busy teachers do, this is demanding, but only in short bursts. Teachers can support each other in such preparation too, swapping ideas and even taking assemblies together. (See Chapter 15, 'Further Suggestions'.)

Generally, it is helpful to link a story/theme/idea with the everyday experiences of the children. This enables you to relate the child to the material and go on to learn from the experiences given in assembly. We all learn in this fashion, building on what we know, reaching into thoughts and concepts, making our own links, answering our own questions.

I aim in this book to give you some detailed examples of assemblies (see Chapter 18), plus strategies to follow and plenty of ideas to develop. If you are an experienced teacher, you may find you prefer to take and develop an item from the list of ideas straight away. If you are less familiar with taking assemblies, perhaps newly qualified, you may decide to try the more prescribed examples to begin with. Then, as you grow in confidence, to go on to the shorter suggestions, and then to take the initiative, looking for your own ideas to work on. This process is all important, because if assemblies are to maintain their vitality they must be geared to your own audience and via your own enthusiasms, linked to this ever-changing world.

The basic principles on which to proceed are, I would suggest –

1. Choose material that supports the teaching of the Bible.
2. Show respect for people, valuing all contributions.
3. Encourage sharing and the participation of the children.
4. Link worship with everyday living and provide variety.
5. Maintain quality, be well prepared, yet adaptable.

It is useful to be on the lookout for ideas all the time, – on your travels, watching TV, meeting new people etc. Collect cuttings from magazines and newspapers, quotations and unusual objects. They may not be of immediate use and inspiration, but you will be surprised how helpful such a personal resource becomes in making assemblies effective and even memorable.

Special Times

I hope looking at the assemblies in this book will not only help you over an immediate hurdle, but also inspire you to greater things, '. . . for cementing people in a group, giving the children something of real quality that a teacher or adult has done for them . . .'[1] is invaluable. Sue Humphries was not referring specifically to assemblies, but she would be correct to speak of them in such terms. They are very vital times in the life of a school. It's worth endeavouring to make each assembly a special time, to which all children are able to respond.

1. Sue Humphries, quoted in Peter Woods, *Creative Teachers in Primary Schools* (Oxford, OUP, 1995) p 84. Sue Humphries is Head of Coombes C.I. and Nursery School, Arborfield, Berkshire.

1 WHAT'S AHEAD

The following pages give you a range of ideas/approaches collected over 14 years in a Junior School, mainly my assemblies with other ideas from about a dozen teachers. Some extra suggestions have been added after my supply teaching in an infant school and consultation with my wife who works there!

As far as I am aware, the ideas are original. Those that I know were taken from other books and sources like the BBC, I have obviously omitted. Very few specific songs or poems are mentioned because the books schools have vary so much and it is a waste of time to spend hours searching – use what you have, and widen the selection as you can.

There are clearly so many different 'types' of assembly. I have categorised those I have experienced, often one led to another as a theme or idea was followed. Bible verses or stories may have been linked with any of these if it helped us to think further. All teachers took turns at leading assembly in our school, the 'senior' ones more often, on a regular basis. Patterns of involvement and frequency were often changed by consultation, and it will be the same in your school.

Our Deputy Head was responsible for the rota and we both kept in touch with all the teachers, dealing with requests and passing on ideas. This is essential and someone must ensure it is done. Teachers should work together to reduce the pressure on each other, not increase it.

Throughout the following sections, **key** or **theme words** are highlighted for quick recognition.

2 QUESTIONING TIMES – A Strategy for All Teachers, not Just Heads

It is becoming common for classes to negotiate and agree their 'rules'. Our assemblies when we posed questions were rather a collaborative approach to finding answers. We, staff and children, had differing opinions and ideas but all were noted – literally. This was one of my favourite approaches and one was never sure where it would lead! But, I am convinced the process was important, not the product, which is more elusive.

>Why do we have **assemblies**?
>What is **worship**?
>How do we know its **springtime**?
>What are **friends** for?
>What makes a good **friend**?
>What is **bullying**?
>What makes a **good school**?
>How can we **care for our surroundings**?
>Let us list some **helpful words** to use e.g. sorry/please.
>What are the **simple pleasures** of life?
>**Healthy** bodies and minds – what helps?
>How do I know I am **growing up**?
>Who are our **heroes** and why?
>What is **temptation**?
>　　　**conscience**?
>　　　**honesty**?
>Why is it good to ask **questions**?!

These were questions posed, often written on a board, a large sheet of paper, or OHP transparency, so the children could start thinking as they arrived in the hall. All suggestions are taken and written up on the list, although similar ones may be amalgamated. What happens, after a time to think on the responses, varies. Children could be asked to put the ideas in order of importance. The list can be written out neatly and/or in large print to reconsider and add to and improve another week. Sometimes we photocopied the lists and sent one to each class for further, more intimate discussion.

I still have many OHP transparencies from these sessions and they make very interesting reading! Teachers joined in as well, sensitively, to keep the ideas coming or to cover an 'unseen angle'. Answers to such questions, honestly accepted, can then be used for further assemblies, either a short talk, a poem, or whatever fits the bill.

Special Times

Warnings –

These assemblies can get lengthy with a large, involved group. So more than one session may be needed, or the item 'delegated' to the class teacher in the meantime if interest is high.

Don't do this too often. Like everything else, over used it can become rather stale. It is great fun though!

Be ready to receive some surprises and not be put off your stride.

Another slight variation on this idea is to ask each class to discuss a topic and bring to the assembly some agreed suggestions.

We often used the formats -

- **Christmas** time is . . .
- **Home** is . . .
- **Friendship** is . . .
- **Happiness** is . . .

Each class is asked to bring, say, three short completions for the sentence, to a designated assembly. Give a few days notice. If one out of six classes forgets, it doesn't matter, and the list can always be left prominently in the hall for completion and further consideration. We found children enjoyed compiling and later referring to these very stimulating lists as the days went by. They did, after all, both belong to and affect us all.

N.B. If you are keen to know some of our 'results', a few are listed in Appendix C on p 84. Later, in a lengthier form, some of these were used in a school anthology of writing.

Another way is to send some questions to each class, compiled perhaps by the older children, when a particular issue needs to be squarely faced and discussed by the whole school.

Relationships at playtime is one area, for example, and on this occasion we asked each class to bring some answers for these questions –

1. What are your favourite playground games?
2. What can we do to improve the playground? (Without requiring stacks of money!)
3. In team games, what do you do if there is an odd number of players; is this solution fair for everyone?
4. Why are people left out of games? How may they feel? What can you do to help?
5. What's enjoyable about team games?
6. List some reasons why games get spoiled in the playground. How can these difficulties be prevented or overcome?

A similar approach, with simpler questions, has been used profitably with infants, on this and other topics of concern, e.g. 'When we play, we . . . ' The children give their ideas, and a list is always a useful reminder. A short, sharp **brainstorming** is also an effective way into such issues, if time is very brief.

3 A POEM OR STORY

There is a wonderful selection of stories and poems for children these days, and many can be employed to provoke thought in assembly. Often it is wise just to use part of a poem to concentrate the focus. Ask questions of the poem yourself, before you decide to use it. Does it fit the theme? Does it provide answers/questions, or both perhaps? Does it stimulate a feeling that can be explored? Is it provoking wonder or hope? It is often helpful to read a short poem several times in assembly, and ask the children to join in from memory, especially if a line is repeated.

Having the words written out or on an OHP transparency is essential if you want the children to say the whole poem all-together, which is a lovely thing to do at times. The poem may well stand on its own, or be part of a wider presentation which it helps to develop. You must select carefully to suit your needs.

Poems

These are some we have found useful over the years:

'Journey back to Christmas', Gwen Dunn, *Oxford Book of Christmas Poems* (Oxford, OUP, 1983) p 76. Lengthy narrative, but valuable for top juniors to ponder the historical events.

'Truth', Barrie Wade, *Oxford Treasury of Children's Poetry* (Oxford, OUP, 1988) p 28 and p 9 of his own anthology *Conkers* (Oxford, OUP).

'Frogspawn – I love it', Bernie Docherty, *Another Third Poetry Book* (Oxford, OUP, 1988) p 97.

'O Great Spirit', Tom Whitecloud, *Story Worlds 2* (London, Oliver and Boyd, 1988) p 49. A prayer from another culture.

'How to Get There', Bonnie Nims, *Another Second Poetry Book* (Oxford, OUP, 1988) p 30. Very good for Mondays and Wednesdays.

'Road of Peace', Paul Robeson, *Wheels Around the World*, compiled by Chris Searle (London, Macdonald, 1983) p 54. A lovely collection of poems from many nations.

'The Tree', Robert Fisher, *Another Second Poetry Book* (Oxford, OUP, 1988) p 10. A useful, powerful quartet of verses for each of the seasons.

'Playground Count', Julie Holder, *Another Second Poetry Book* (Oxford, OUP, 1988) p 20. New term or recognising differences, what I call a 'Yuk and Yippee' theme, i.e. good and bad, pros and cons.

'Spring Nature Notes', Ted Hughes. Parts of it as you require, e.g. 'March morning unlike any other'. From his *Seasons Songs* anthology (London, Faber, 1995). Also in Fiona Waters' anthology *Out of the Blue* (London, Collins Lions).

'Excuses', Allan Ahlberg, *Please, Mrs. Butler* (London, Puffin, 1984) p 61.

'Autumn – not ours, Lord, but yours', Donald Hilton, *A Word in Season* (Birmingham, NCEC, 1990) p 133.

'Christmas Thank you's', Mick Gowar, *Oxford Book of Christmas Poems* (Oxford, OUP, 1983)

Special Times

p 134.

'Picking Teams' and 'The Runners', Allan Ahlberg, *Against the Odds* (Bucks, GINN, 1989) pp 4, 72. Short, amusing and to the point.

Knowing Yourself, 'I seem to be . . . but I really am', Jeff Morley, *Into Poetry* by Richard Andrews (London, Ward Lock Educational, 1983) p 76.

'In the Dark', June Pridmore, *Poetry Plus 4, Green Earth and Silver Stars*, (Huddersfield, Schofield & Sims, 1983) p 11.

'The Quarrel', Mark Winyard, *Wheels Around the World* (London, Macdonald, 1983) p23.

'Problems', Brian Moses, *Green Poetry*, edited by Robert Hull (Hove, Wayland, 1991) p 8. Useful in tackling environmental issues.

'Leisure', William H Davies, *Delight & Warnings*, John & Gillian Beer (London, Macdonald, 1984) p 68. One to ponder and return to.

'A Useful Person', Kit Wright, *Hot Dogs* (London, Puffin, 1982) p 20. A good starter into the subject of 'handicap'/educationally challenged, and developing ourselves.

'Splashing through the puddles', Lydia Pender, *Morning Magpie* (Lancaster, Angus and Robertson, 1984) p 15.

'The Silent Witnesses', Frank Topping, *Pause for Thought* (Cambridge, Lutterworth, 1981)

There is also a list in Appendix A of poetry books which hold a wealth of material that can be used to link with themes, instigate discussion or stand on their own as thought-provokers.

Stories

A selection we have found helpful over the years. These may well need to be read in more than one assembly, and can be used for further investigation at different levels and for various purposes in class activities. Parts can be summarised, as you see fit.

A. Thinking about human characters, their needs and feelings

'Adolf', D. H. Lawrence, *Thoughtscapes*, edited by Barry Maybury (Oxford, OUP, 1972) p 70. (Not what you may think! – have a look).
Alfie Gets Back First, Shirley Hughes (London, Collins Picture Lions, 1981).
Alfie gives a hand, Shirley Hughes (London, Collins Picture Lions, 1983).
An evening at Alfie's, Shirley Hughes (London, Collins Picture Lions, 1984).
Dogger, Shirley Hughes, (Norwich, Red Fox, 1983).
Eddie the Elephant Stephanie Jeffs (Wiltshire, Tamarind, 1993).
Folktales Joan Aiken (London, Puffin, 1981), out of print, but worth seeking.
'His First Flight', Liam O'Flaherty, *Wordscapes*, edited by Barry Maybury (Oxford, OUP, 1970) p 62.
Kirsty's Kite, Carol Curtis Stilz (Oxford, Albatross Books, 1988).
Martin is our Friend one of a series on caring for the physically and educationally challenged (London, Methuen,1980).
Mog & Bunny, Judith Kerr (London, Collins Picture Lions, 1991).
Mog the Forgetful Cat, Judith Kerr (London, Collins Picture Lions, 1991).
Joseph's Yard, Charles Keeping (Oxford, OUP, 1969).
More about Paddington, Michael Bond (London, Penguin, 1971).
Princess Smarty Pants, Babette Cole (Londo, Armada, 1986).
Roberto and the Magical Fountain, Donna Reid Vann (Oxford, Lion Publishing, 1988).

Stephan's Secret Fear, Donna Reid Vann (Oxford, Lion Publishing, 1990).
Tale of Three Trees, Angela Elwell Hunt (Oxford, Lion Publishing, 1989).
The Lark Who Had No Song, Carolyn Nystrom (Oxford, Lion Publishing, 1991).
The Marble Crusher, Michael Morpurgo (London, Macmillan, 1992).
The Very Worried Sparrow, Meryl Doney (Oxford, Lion Publishing, 1979).
Wind in the Willows, Kenneth Grahame (London, Harper Collins, 1995), chapter 4, 'Mole in the wild wood', re. fear/loneliness.
The Book of Heroic Failures, Stephen Pile (London, Futura, 1980). A collection of true stories, many humorous.

B. Our relationhips with each other and God

Series of Jungle Doctor Fables:

Rhino Rumblings, Paul White (Exeter, Paternoster Press, 1974).
Hippo Happenings, Paul White (Exeter, Paternoster Press, 1972).
Monkey Tales, Paul White (Exeter, Paternoster Press, 1972).
Tug-of-war, (Exeter, Paternoster Press, 1972).

Moral parables with talking animals. Not everyone's choice but great fun and revealing. I recommend 'names' are abbreviated or not used, for ease of reading. Still very popular with the children. Out of print, but worth seeking second hand.

The Selfish Giant, Oscar Wilde (London, Picture Puffins, Penguin, 1982).
'The Watch' by Michael Rosen, from *Quick, Let's Get Out of Here*, his own collection (London, Puffin, 1985) p 33.
Vet in a Spin, James Herriott (London, Pan, 1978) pp 92–96. Hilarious events and the need to say sorry.
Aesop's Fables – available in many versions.
Haffertee series by Janet and John Perkins (Oxford, Lion, 1989), adventures of a loveable soft-toy hamster.
Some Greek legends – if you like them, and can retell them with clarity.

C Longer stories that Juniors enjoy as a serial, or excerpts, and valuable for raising issues:-

Boy, Roald Dahl (London, Penguin, 1984).
Elephants don't sit on cars, David Henry Wilson (London, Piccolo, 1980).
Folk Tales, Leila Berg (London, Brockhampton Press, 1966). Also available in 'Take Part' series (Sussex, Ward Lock, 1976).
Gaffer Samson's Luck, Jill Paton Walsh (London, Puffin, 1987).
Julian Stories, Ann Cameron (London, Young Lions, 1994).
The Goalkeepers Revenge and Other Stories, Bill Naughton (London, Penguin, 1970).
The Iron Man, Ted Hughes (London, Faber, 1968).

Some old favourites that need preparation and editing are also very worth considering, e.g. Just-so Stories by Rudyard Kipling, and some of the Arabian Nights stories: 'The King and the Fisherman' as a start.

4 LOOK, LISTEN AND . . . ?

Looking

When the children come into the hall for assembly it takes a little time. It is best to have something for them to do straight away. An unknown visitor sitting at the front for them to weigh up is probably the most potent, or it was for our school!

The key here is a variety. Based on a routine expectation, we used –

- **OHP** to display-
    - a message/thought/question
    - title to the assembly
    - details of music playing (if any)
    - a short poem or saying
    - a picture to ponder

Note: Some teachers suggested a collection of pictures for the OHP would be useful. We've done our best to start you off! Our selection, with some starting points, forms Chapter 16.

- **A picture or pictures to look at**. Many good prints are available now of the work of famous and not so famous artists. Children's paintings, a teacher's from home, something from the local museum/resources centre are other options. A few words about what 'looking' at a picture might mean is essential from time to time! If convenient for you, the picture may take the form of a slide. I remember once a teacher placed on a stand one of her own unfinished oil paintings and how enthralled the children were as they sat and looked! She went on to explain that paintings, like writing, often have to be left a while and returned to, in order not only to 'finish' it but to get the best result.

Guide the children to look at a detail, enjoy the colours etc. If there are several pictures ask them to look at each in turn to see what they are about, or consider how they react to the images.

- **Objects** are the most common items to focus attention. I have seen used –

    Flowers – sometimes one rose, sometimes an abundance
    Candles – Lit in a safe situation
    Blossoms – of various types
    Leaves and patterns of them
    Live pets (including a teacher's two dogs who just lay there and helped us all to relax!)
    A child or person sitting and doing something

Look, Listen and . . . ?

Bicycles
Giant pine cones
A large kite

Children are curious, and having the object in a bag, or large laundry basket, and walking up and down looking perplexed, whispering 'I wonder what's in here?' is a winner.

Don't make life too difficult for yourself! All sorts of things can be used, and others are mentioned elsewhere on specific themes. Something/anything that grabs the attention and sets the mind going is a great help.

Proximity is sometimes a problem, but trial and error is the only way to sort it out. I have seen 200 plus children comfortably sitting in the round looking quietly, and also the same number requiring two of everything raised on boxes, one on each side of the hall – all down to the design of the building.

Listening

We didn't always play music as the children entered assembly. I know many schools do and that's fine. For us absolute silence coming into the hall was not a daily requirement, but when music was played we did want everyone to listen, not just have it there as background sounds. I would suggest a variety of approaches helps to maintain discipline and provoke involvement.

• **Music** When played as the children entered, we often put a question about it on the OHP, e.g. which instruments can you recognise? how does it make you feel? Music used otherwise, for example, to centre our attention during the actual assembly, was just as common. Some ideas that we tried are listed here. I urge you to have the music on a cassette or CD, rather than try to find a section on a record efficiently.

Volunteer children playing live music is another option you may have available to provide a new dimension as well. This could lead to a whole series of assemblies on **talents**.

Incidentally, a really effective use of music at the start of assembly is to be singing a song and as the children enter they sit and join in!

Recorded music to use during assembly, to listen to and perhaps lead into or be an integral part of the talk or theme:

- 'I did it my way', Frank Sinatra – which we used in order to say it was better to 'give and take' than do it 'our way'.
- 'Listen, do you wanna know a secret?', Beatles.
- 'Money, Money, Money', Abba. Used with OHP transparency No 1.
- 'Spread a little happiness', Sting.
- 'Together', Julian Bream and John Williams (two guitars heard as one).
- From Walt Disney's *Jungle Book* film 'Trust in me', hypnotic melody from the cunning Ka, the snake!
- Garth Hewitt – (an international troubadour). 'Water, Water' and 'Nero's Watching Video' from his album *Road to Freedom*.
- John Pantry, 'Yours is such a strong love'. A singer/writer whose songs often hit the nail on the head. This song has a line – 'my head so full of noise and my mouth so full of words, I didn't know the right from the wrong'. (From album,'*Empty handed*).
- *Scheherazade* – Sinbad's ship at sea – Rimsky Korsakov.

Special Times

To listen to and just sit and enjoy together:

- 'Be Still' – classical praise guitar, Rob and Gilly.
- 'Flight of the Condor', Sumaj Rumi (Bolivian group).
- 'Jazz Sebastian Bach', Swingle Singers (old and new).
- 'Mr. Mistoffelees', from *Cats* musical.
- 'Together', Julian Bream and John Williams, guitar duets.
- Acker Bilk, jJazz on a clarinet.
- Beatles songs played by Tijuana Brass.
- Cambridge Buskers, 'Double Concerto'.
- Duane Eddy – old favourites on guitar.
- Eric Satie piano pieces.
- James Galway plays Chopin.
- John William's theme from *Schindler's List*.
- Mozart, Concerto in C major for flute and harp.
- 'Straight from the heart of Africa', Kagando choir (Tear Fund).
- Vivaldi, *The Four Seasons*.

Plus so much more that you can employ imaginatively. You get the idea! Music shops have a good ordering service these days, as do our public libraries.

•**Sound Effects** provide another way to get everyone to listen attentively either at the start of or during assembly. As well as the many cassettes and records produced, children can invent their own, and many keyboards have pre-set selections these days too. Carefully chosen sounds are very good for getting into a certain frame of mind (running water?) or another world (eerie noises). Keep them short though, with clear instructions to the children.

It is also good just to sit and listen in 'silence', especially on a warm day with the windows open, to the world outside. Many avenues of interest to follow there, according to your own surroundings.

5 SHORT TALKS – A Hundred and More Starting Points

The teacher(s), finally, are the crux of all this and, quite rightly, provide words with the objects, music, demonstration or picture, that also demand attention. Whatever you are utilising in your assembly, your rapport with the children is crucial. Vary your pace, your voice, watch their reaction, make your expectations clear in any given situation. Learn too from the other teachers around you.

The talk you give has to be thought through. What follows is a list of suggestions, all employed by teachers, for you to consider. Some teachers ask for a lot of guidance, some for just the embryo of an idea, we are all different. So the amount of information offered here varies considerably. I am convinced that all teachers are creative, so you are sure to find something you can take and re-shape into a lovely assembly! An assembly which may involve worship and wonder in a very meaningful way.
   If you require a detailed presentation to use quickly, have a look now at Chapter 18.
   Here are some short-talk ideas we used effectively – add your own 'flesh to the bone'. I hope these notes provide sparks that will inspire you.

- 'To **learn** something new you have to take a risk' – is this true, do you think? Give some examples and ask for more.
- 'What can I take **credit** for?' – my nose, the price of my shoes? The way I behave, my attitude to people and work?
- 'If you want a **friend**, be a friend' . . . What does this mean?
- '**Keep it up** two, three, four . . . five, six' (perhaps using Elephant's song from *Jungle Book*). A good start +? . . . perseverance is a lovely word to introduce! Explain, and ask what do you think must follow?
- 'Our **habits** – good and bad.' Do we know what they are? How can we change them?
- '**Rules**, rules – where would a game of cricket be without them?' What rules bring us benefit?
- '**Love** is something that if you give it away, you end up having more.' Examples from family life. Perhaps use the catchy song. 'Magic Penny' in *Allelujah!* (A & C Black).
- Handmade **cards**, home-made **presents** and **simple treasures**. Three teachers followed this theme quite impromptu, sharing their reaction to special presents.
- The **white dove** – bring a picture in paint or words. The symbol and the reality, peace in our world and lives today.
- A **Global Village**? – using a world map and news cuttings, reinforce the oneness of human beings, our shared needs.
- Bring a message on a **T-shirt** (I had 'No Problem', 'Don't put a hole in the world' and 'I don't do mornings'). Children have many too!
- 'You can't **judge** a book by its cover' – give examples. Apply it to people, how easily we can be deceived.

Special Times

- **Footprints** worth following – cut out some feet and arrange them to go behind a cupboard or out of a door where something of 'value' is found. Give an example of your choice of someone worth learning from/following/emulating.
- 'Be a **good sport**', explain to each other what this means.
- '**Small** is beautiful' (Dr E. F. Schumacher) . . . is this true? . . . always?
- '**People** we love, things we use', 'people are more important than things.' Explain together.
- Birds can fly high, but people need **space** too, both physically and mentally. Don't they? How do we provide it for each other?
- 'Any **excuse** is better than none'. Do you agree and why?
- 'Engage brain before opening **mouth**.' Why is this so vital?
- 'Two ears, one mouth – **listen** and speak in those proportions.'
- 'Get your **facts** right first.' Share stories illustrating how this is important.
- Ask the children what they really have **control** over in their lives – diet/watching TV/reading/habits/attitudes/rest/exercise/hobbies/thinking/temper/affections? It may amaze them how much more they could do and who is responsible! Each area lends itself to further investigation.
- **Memory** skills – how good are yours? Use large items in Kim's Game for all to enjoy. Reflect on long and short term abilities. One to remember to come back to.
- **Our five senses** – how do we use them to gather information?
- **Holiday** memories . . . teachers and children have happy/worrying/exciting moments.
- Coping with our **worries**. How do we do it?
- Favourite **books** – ask a few children to talk about their personal choices.
- 'Some like **noise** and din, others love peace and quiet.' Which are you? How can such different people get along rubbing shoulders, day by day?
- **Calm** – Careful – Considerate. Meeting people like that all day long is great! Seek explanations and share examples and incidents.
- 'Expect from yourself, what you expect from others.'
- Chinese Whispering Game. Problems and strategies of getting the **message**.
- 'Looking up, **optimism**, and looking down, **pessimism**' – a place for both? What will today bring? How can we alter our attitudes?
- **Milestones** – in my/your/our lives. Looking back and forward.
- '**Seeds** of the **Spirit**' (from 'Light up the fire' song, BBC *Come and Praise* No 55) – ponder on its meaning. Ask for ideas (some are in the song); refer to Paul's words in Galatians 5 verse 23; look at seeds, plant them. What comes between planingt and the fruit? **Growth** – a long-term lesson here. How do we achieve it?
- 'Joy grows in the soil of praise' – see Psalm 148.
- **Dreams** – what are they? Refer to Joseph or Daniel. Share some together, if you wish. In planning for life will 'any dream do?!' Some Aboriginal art and music fits in nicely here.
- **Spring** and **New Year** customs in other countries (e.g. Chinese Dragon Dance) and other times (e.g. a Victorian village). (See Appendix A booklist.)
- **Balancing** – demonstrate concept with scales or equaliser. What does this show us? Accurate weight or number. Other balances in life – in gymnastics, 'the books', and in nature (food chains). All bringing health and safety. Imbalance is dangerous! What does this teach us about life? List ideas.
- **Looking ahead** – ask a few children to say what they want to do when they grow up. Spend a few quiet moments thinking on the future and what we can do to shape it.
- **Fads and fancies.** Note how they come and go.
- '**Knowledge is Power**'. Discuss if this is true, giving examples.
- 'The **computer** above our eyebrows' – the wonder of our brains – thinking, remembering, planning etc. etc. Yet it has limitations – 'my thoughts are higher than your thoughts, says the Lord'.

- The Futility of **war** . . . Look at a topical example.
- 'Do your own think.' The importance of **thinking** things through.
- '**People** are like the blossom – beautiful up on the tree, a real bother when they drop and get under your feet.' If we feel like this, how can we help each other – in school, at home and in the wider world?
- **Distractions** – what are they? Read 'Distracted the mother said to her boy' (*Oxford Fourth Poetry Book* by Gregory Harrison, p 9). Worth developing with older Juniors.
- **Changes** – the weather, the circumstances at school, perhaps at home. Hold on to the essential things in order to cope. What are they? How are we changing ourselves? Sometimes we have to change to fit in!
- '**Life** is for living.' What does this mean to us?
- The **Poppy Appeal** . . . explain purpose.
- **Time** – what is it? Ways of measuring it. 'Time is the thief of youth', use each day wisely. 'Our times are in God's hands', keep things in proportion. We only have each day once.
- Our favourite **toys** — bring in a few to share.
- Show **slides** – as large as possible, perhaps on a wall, of another country (just 4 or 5). You or a friend may have some holiday snaps. If not there are various suppliers (see Appendix B). Gently talk through them and answer questions. Pause to remember the people and their needs today.
- My **friends** – do I value them as I should? 'A friend in need, is a friend indeed' – unravel this for the children! 'Greater love has no man than this, that he lays down his life for his friends'. . . Jesus is the supreme example, but some people have emulated Him over the centuries.
- 'A worry **shared** is a worry halved' (my version!).
- 'Getting to **the top**' – e.g. climbing Mount Everest, or what? Only a few can be the very best, and what's there when you reach the summit? Jack Higgins (best selling thriller writer) said 'nothing'. So does Boris Becker apparently.
- Introducing the school **pets** – our responsibility for them.
- Who is a good **discoverer/finder/collector**? Investigate how and why together. Bring in examples.
- The mirror – how well do I use it?! Apply to the physical, then widen the issues (refer to James 1:23–24 in Bible) and see how accurately we view ourselves. 'Warts and all' – like Cromwell?
- '**Progress**' – what is it for me? For the school?
- 'Put yourself in the **other person's shoes**.' Think an example through in detail and add some humour.
- **Road Sign** – borrow one! Yes, a real one. e.g. 'Road Narrows' or 'Men at Work'. Ask – what does it mean, where shall we be able to place it around the school today? Be creative ...
- 'Of the making of **books**, there is no end.' Examine why and rejoice in a selection. A really old one is a bonus.
- Simple **crossword** – as an aide-memoire; compile one on a theme and go through it as a school, completing say 5/6 clues. A good way to look back over a few assemblies. Note any deviant thinking for future assemblies!
- '**Friends** are for sharing, not owning.'
- Real **friends** sometimes **say No** . . . Why is this?
- **Father Christmas**, Santa Claus, Saint Nicholas – look at the various traditions around Europe. Try to distil 'the essence' of them.
- 'The Lord is **My Shepherd**.'
- 'All life is **learning**.'
- **A message** on one hand/a five finger tale. As it happens the above quote from Psalm 23 is one! Use your hand, finger by finger, to say each word and then revise the message

Special Times

together. This can be re-done as often as you like, according to age and necessity. E.g. always do your very best/be kind to one another.
- **'A smile** goes a long way' . . . What does this mean, try it!
- **Goodwill** – has to be seen in action.
- Build a **wall** of wooden bricks, with three/four bricks strategically chosen that are loose. So when your volunteers come out one by one, to remove a brick, the wall gradually collapses. An exciting experience in itself! I use this to portray **Peter** the Apostle, before (strong and firm) and after (broken and remorseful) his denial of Jesus. Then go on to read from one of his letters (perhaps 2 Peter 1.1–4) to show his experience didn't end there, he was 'rebuilt' and strengthened. We build the wall even better the second time.
This illustration may well fit another idea of your own too.
- Read slowly a **Christmas** greeting card from Bethlehem itself. (Write to me if you want one!)
- Use a **poster** of an aerial (satellite) photograph of our planet **Earth**. Give children a few actual measurements of its real size. Can we find our islands on it? 'We are just a pin-prick' as people. This one planet, of one solar system, of one galaxy, out of probably millions – the vastness of it all. Yet God cares for us all (cf. Psalm 19:.1, Psalm 8:3–4).
- 'Don't jump to conclusions' . . . a negative instruction, but so very necessary. Show why. Ask children for daily examples of **misunderstandings** that could have been avoided.
- Investigating **parcels** – there are many purposes and messages in this activity.
- 'Like a **tree** planted by the water side, we shall not be moved' – yes, Anfield's old war cry, but do we realise that the picture comes from Psalm 1, and refers to God's provision, now and forever, for those who follow His way? (A large picture of a tree with roots and branches is a help.)
- **Salt** – so simple, but we cannot do without it. Give some idea of its uses over the centuries, and its value. You can stop here, or go on to link this with Jesus' description of His disciples as salt (Matt 5:13). What does this mean for us today?
- **Waste** and **recycling** in our school – evaluate, draw up an action plan corporately. A long-term theme.
- The **probables** and **possibles** of life – help each other to tell them apart!
- What's new? – for beginning of year, or term, ask children and teachers for observations on any **changes** to building/grounds/arrangements that make life better. Be thankful for them, perhaps write letters as appropriate.
- Michaelmas, Candlemas – what are the other 'Quarters' of **the year**? Explain their derivation and use the words of yesteryear as the new year glides by.
- 'Bare **Necessities of Life**' – what do we think they are? Perhaps play Baloo's song from *Jungle Book* and note his character. Is the 'simple life' more satisfying or not? You may like to turn this into a series and look at lifestyles in an African village/a mid-European Gypsy camp and so on. Do we 'count our blessings'?
- **Mazes** – explain what they are; ask for any experiences of being in one. Labyrinths, Puzzles. Working with a new computer program is like that at first. Life is full of puzzles. Think about them and seek help from outside ourselves. Where can we turn?
- How **generous** are we? Read parable of vineyard workers (Matt 20) and look at why some moaned while others were happily surprised.
- BC and AD. He changed the **calendar**! (For most of the world's population) . . . Explain the meanings and how we count backwards and forwards from the Great Event of History, the birth of Jesus.
- 'It is wise to follow the **maker's instructions**'. Linked with a personal experience e.g. buying and beginning to use a new washing machine, or when the car wouldn't start, point out that we should turn to the manual, the maker's instructions. These tell us how to get the best out of our machines, how to treat them, maintain them, and when they break

down, mend them.

The opening story can be as graphic as you like, which then makes the application more powerful. How silly to ignore the maker's instructions! God is our Maker, and He has given us instructions. Refer to the 10 Commandments (Exodus. 20) or Jesus' teaching in Matthew 5 & 6 (Sermon on the Mount). A particular point can be made (e.g. our need to forgive one another) or a general one – 'Love God with all your heart, and your neighbour as yourself' (Jesus' own resume of the Law).

'So to get the best out of life, don't wait until things go wrong, take heed of a loving Creator's advice.'

This presupposes a belief in God and the truth of the Bible, of course, plus a reliance on a power beyond ourselves.

- **Nicknames** – what do they tell us about each other? Good or bad? Give or share some examples. Recall, long ago 'Christians' was only a rude, unkind nickname, meaning 'Christ's people'. (See Acts 11:26.)
- **Excuses** or reasons? Examine the differences in day to day situations. Is honesty the key?
- This is me! Ask each child to bring a black and white sketch of themselves/self portrait into assembly. These can be collected and mounted all around the hall. Talk about **individuality**, how we perceive ourselves, and other interesting points.
- Commemorative **stamps** – use a set to open up a subject for the whole school.
- 'Keeping up **appearances**' – perhaps some children will know the TV series. Introduce the issues involved and relate them to real-life values/motives.
- **Focus** – a good thing to do at times. Why? What does it mean for different situations?
- **'Give us a clue!'** Play the game together, with an object in a box. Arrange your own rules. With time and practice the children can run this too and you only need to be ready with your 'punch-line'.
- Create **an A, B, C,** on a theme e.g. for Advent – Angels, Baby, Choirs . . . or for protecting the environment – Alternatives, Biodegradable, Cans . . . Plenty of useful discussion points here.
- **'Quality** is more important than **quantity'**?!
- Cut a large **fruit** in half – look at the patterns inside. What else is there? . . . Seeds, for future crops, new life hidden there. 'Seeing to the **heart of the matter**' means what is really there, often not noticed at first, often very hopeful.

Finally, in this vein, a few quotations from the book of Proverbs for consideration as short 'sound-bite' assemblies -

- VALUE
  Wisdom is more profitable than silver and yields better returns than gold (3:14).
- CONCENTRATION
  Let your eyes look straight ahead. Fix your gaze directly before you (4:25). (Not only applicable to Blondin as he crossed Niagara!)
- TINY BUT?
  Go to the ant, consider its ways and be wise (6:6). (Another link with team work.)
- THE TONGUE
  Hatred stirs up dissension, but love covers over all wrongs (10:12 see also 17:9).
- SMILES
  A cheerful heart is good medicine (17:22).
- ACTIONS
  Even a child is known by his/her actions (20:11).

If these ancient quotations have fascinated you, why not look for some more, here and elsewhere?

6 CLASS-LED ASSEMBLIES

These were usually a celebration and sharing of work recently accomplished, with perhaps a little 'message' woven-in. Originally they were quite frequent and as the school grew, we agreed one class assembly for each class each year was sufficient.

Most teachers will be familiar with this type of assembly. Perhaps a child or children will do the introducing. Writing, pictures, maps, models, music, drama, news of visits, even gymnastics would be presented to the school. Although rehearsed to some extent we never wanted the assembly to be a 'performance' solely, however enjoyable. Nor did we wish any competitive element to creep-in, as it so easily can, between classes. These are dangers, and I think by having these assemblies well spread out – in the end two or three a term – and discussing our attitudes as a staff, we avoided the pitfalls.

Once the school returned to roughly the number for which the building had been designed (280) we then had the chance to invite the parents of each class to come and share in the occasions. Tea and biscuits, served by the children with the help of a classroom assistant, were always available afterwards. Such events provided an opportunity for all the children to be involved in presenting an assembly. Parents enjoyed their visits and many found closer links with the school through them, some going on to take part in assemblies themselves!

Often too, teachers would involve their classes, or a group, in other assemblies for which they were responsible. I, as Headteacher, was always ready to fit in requests from the children, and on the look-out for writing, pictures or ideas that would support the theme of an assembly. You may wish to involve all or some of your class in preparing another sort of assembly, one with a spiritual or moral message.

Brainstorming round a theme is an excellent start. The ideas noted can then be followed through and discussed in more detail. Challenge the children as to how the point can be effectively presented, for example:

Envy
    discuss what it is,
    try to define it,
    share examples,
    choose a story to tell (real or imaginary),
    how can we fight it?

Use the children's own words and suggestions so they communicate their thoughts and feelings to the rest of the school. This approach can be applied to so many themes.

Alternatively, to enable everyone to recognise and rejoice in diversity, collect some **class statistics**. These are facts not opinions or interpretations. Height, hair colour, span, weight, arm length, shoe size, house number etc. All can be collected and charted. Be wary of going into areas that can be sensitive for some families, e.g. type of car!

These can all be presented objectively in assembly. Perhaps children who wish to could take in self-portraits to add to the visual effect. Children can make observations from these facts, perhaps pose questions, e.g. why are there so few blue-eyed children in class 6? Whatever you think fits.

The point is, we are all so different – and matters of taste in food, hobbies, feelings, experiences haven't been entered into at all – yet. 'But,' you can say, 'we all work together as a class.' Now, or later, examples can be given of how they help each other out, day by day.

You may find the 'About me' photocopiable sheet (p 86) useful here, or in a similar activity. Each child, either in a group or class, is asked to write five facts about him/herself. The children then share with each other, as they choose. Prayers rejoicing in their differences can be compiled. Limiting the amount to be written encourages thought and makes the task accessible.

7 VISITORS

I presume most primary schools, like ours, are regularly asked by charity representatives if they could speak at an assembly? Not all however requested a fund-raising activity afterwards, and many still came to speak about their work without any promise of money. So, it is possible to keep control, and be selective. We thought this was a reasonable addition to our regular assemblies once each half-term at a maximum. Children are always ready to help in these ways, even without personal incentives like badges! It is good for them too, to learn firsthand, as it were, of the needs of others.

Some of our better regular speakers over a four-year span, came from Sightsavers, Barnardo's, Children's Society, NSPCC, National Children's Homes, Leprosy Action, Shaftesbury Society, British Red Cross and our local Hospice. Many bring slides and very useful information packs. But clearly you are dependent on what is available locally and governed by how often you wish to be involved. Your own interests may lead your school to seek out visitors from a local wildlife trust or a band from the Salvation Army. The scope is endless, but arranging things may take quite a lot of time.

Speakers from local churches – not always ministers – retired missionaries and overseas aid workers were often very good at addressing the children, bringing a new perspective to life and up-to-date information from around the world. If you have willing people from other faiths they could come and talk about their religion too. A nearby university may help with students from different cultures who are capable of speaking to children. Many, we found, were keen to visit an English school and some were prepared to stay quite a while after the assembly and even return to foster further links.

8 LINKS WITH THE WIDER COMMUNITY

Through visiting our assemblies, a lot of people in our village community were able to keep us informed of their own activities and maintain links with the school in many ways. These were visitors whom we knew, came in more often, and whom the children could also meet at other times around the school or in the local area.

All neighbourhood police and fire officers like to talk regularly with children in schools. In addition local shop and factory workers, children's librarian, mums and dads with skills to display, school doctor, governors, officers from local clubs (e.g. over 60s and Horticultural), Council officials, the lollipop lady, Grans and Grandads with memories to share . . . all these and many more provide a wonderful source of help for assemblies. Most people are quite happy to keep within an allotted time! Make sure the 'brief' is crystal clear, though.

Once they have been, the secret is to pick up and use something said or shown by the visitor and develop the theme whilst the children are enthused. Then be ready for the next visitor!

Assembly too was a time when we welcomed new staff to the school and presented gifts to those leaving. What the new MDA or the retiring teacher says to the children will often stick in their minds and give inspiration for further assemblies.

Linking these everyday events, the real-life situations of people, with the teaching and worship of assemblies is valuable, making pertinent what otherwise may be too theoretical. Be on the lookout for ideas, at all times when the school is gathered, and lead by example.

9 LEARNING NEW SONGS

We were always fortunate to have able, dedicated and enthusiastic teachers to lead the musical life of the school. As one succeeded the other, they each built on what went before and brought their own extra ingredient to bear. **Singing practices** with hundreds of children are lively times and ours were no exception. Both discipline and enjoyment are essential, and these were certainly provided. A regular time was set aside each week for learning new songs. Unusual words or phrases were explained to the children, so, hopefully, they understood a bit more of what they were singing. Encouraged to do so, children will ask questions also about the relevance of what we teach them, not always at times convenient to us!

Some songs are meditative, some very lively. All must be reasonably easy for teachers and children to pick up quickly. It's far better if everyone can join in enthusiastically. Songs are excellent starting points for an assembly. These we found went very well –

'**Wake up**, each day sun shining through', which has many useful thoughts within it about **using time** to the full and searching for satisfaction. (*Allelujah!*, London, A&C Black, 1960, song 60).

'Light up the fire', a **community** song that points us to Jesus (*BBC – Come and Praise*, London, 1978, song 55).

Graham Kendrick's very popular '**Shine** Jesus Shine', beginning 'Lord the Light of your love is shining . . .' (song 120 in *Let's Praise*, Basingstoke, Marshall Pickering, 1988).

'Lord, I love to stamp and shout . . .' (*Someone's Singing Lord*, London, A&C Black, 1973, song 4). A whole catalogue of **verbs** that can be highlighted and discussed.

'Streets of London', awareness of other's needs(song 41 in *Allelujah!* A&C Black).

'I can climb the highest mountain . . .' **talents** recognised and 'Happy to be me' (*Every colour under the sun*, London, Ward Lock, 1983, song 17).

'**Think** of a world without any flowers', **thankfulness** that these things are here (*BBC – Come and Praise*, London, 1978, song 17).

'The **Building** song', first line 'All over the world . . .' (*BBC – Come and Praise*, London 1978, song 61 and *Allelujah!* A&C Black, song 59).

'One More **Step**', Sydney Carter's song with obvious applications at beginning and end of term (*BBC – Come and Praise*, London, 1978, song 47).

'Cross over the road, my friend . . .' The need for **action** not just words (*BBC Come and Praise*, London, 1978, song 70).

Learning New Songs

'There are hundreds of sparrows', or 'hundreds and thousands' (*Sing to God*, song 18, London, Scripture Union). Very effective with cubes or squares to show a million – how vast the **universe** is and what a God who made it!

'Thank you, **Thank you** Lord for this new day' (*BBC – Come and Praise*, London, 1978, song 32).

'**Christmas** time is fruit and wine . . .' (Penelope's carol in the *Oxford Christmas Book for Children*, OUP).

A further list of songbooks appears in Appendix B. Also some songs are linked in the text with particular assemblies.

Everyone has their own favourites of course, and some are peculiar to one or two schools only I've found! I think the secret of achieving balance and variety, with so many things, is for as many people to be involved in the selection as possible.

All children and teachers should be able to suggest new songs, but with the one who has to teach the music having the final say. We found this worked quite sensibly. A list of OHP transparencies was kept, so all those responsible for assemblies could choose what to sing and ask for it to be practised, if they wished.

Something else we did that may appeal to you is to **write our own words** to a given tune. Any child, group or class could then have a try. A very well-known and popular song tune would be used, e.g. 'Autumn days when the grass is jewelled' (*BBC – Come and Praise*), and we wrote words for the other seasons as the year progressed. This provides an excellent task for the children and new lively and special verses. Some help from a teacher may be necessary at times to fit the words in properly! You may even be fortunate enough, as we were, to have musical pupils who are able to completely write their own songs.

10 RETELLING BIBLE STORIES

You would expect (if you have read the Introduction) that I made sure this was done. The quest for truth and reality is something all people share. It is a serious mission and Jesus said, 'I am the Truth' (John 14:6) and 'God's word is truth' (John 17:17). So this ingredient in our feast of assemblies could not be omitted! I would suggest when reading from the Bible that the Good News, New International and Contemporary English versions are best.

The stories though must be made pertinent to the children. Re-telling a worthwhile story is a valuable experience for everyone anyway and sometimes that's all I did. In other instances I would introduce the tale with a bit of background, or a relevant question. For help with valuable authentic details and biblical background material that is easy to assimilate use the *Lion Handbook to the Bible*. Otherwise, I might ask at the end what the children learned from the story, or how a certain character felt in the situation. In any event, I made it clear that I believed its historicity and applicability to life, and that each of them had to make up their own minds as time went by. My task was to sow the seed – in an interesting way.

I admit, this took time – one must read and re-read the Bible account to ensure accuracy and open-up the event to further thought and comments that are applicable in making it realistic. You must keep it lively! I was amazed though how well some stories 'went down' and the after-flow they created, to pose questions and provide further topics to follow up.

Some Old Testament stories

- Creation. **Genesis 1 & 2**
- Noah and the Ark. **Genesis 6–9**.
- Abraham's Journeys. **Genesis 12–13**.
- Moses leads the people. **Exodus 13–18**.
- Joseph – all or some! **Exodus 37–45**.
- Battle of Jericho. Plus song? **Joshua 6**.
- Deborah. **Judges 4 & 5**.
- Gideon. **Judges 7**.
- David – Shepherd/Soldier/King. Beginning **1 Samuel 16** and Mephibosheth (yes! when looked at, a lovely story of reconciliation – see **2 Samuel 9**).
- Josiah and the lost scrolls **2 Chronicles 34**.
- **Jonah** and the whale/big fish.
- **Ruth**.
- **Nehemiah** and the new wall.
- **Esther** – certainly a different culture.
- **Daniel**.

For younger primaries, Nick Butterworth and Mick Inkpen's *Stories Jesus Told* are a delight (London, Harper Collins 1991–1995). Several Arch Books are very readable too published by Concordia (if still available, worth seeking out in jumble sales if not!) on Naaman, Moses, Zacchaeus, Two Men in the Temple and The Rich Fool, as are most of *The Lion Story Bible* series – 50 titles in all. (Oxford, Lion, 1983 onwards).

New Testament stories

There are so many that are fine for re-telling, most of them from the life of Jesus. 'Musts' are the Sower (**Luke 8:1–15**) and the Lost Sheep (**Luke 15**), Zacchaeus (**Luke 19:1-9**) and the Feeding of the 5,000 (**John 6:1–15**).

An excellent book is published by Lion, *Stories of Jesus* by Timothy Dudley-Smith. This is the one book I know that tells the stories accurately and in a fashion very acceptable to be read verbatim to today's children. Somehow they appeal.

Other stories lend themselves very well to simple drama, e.g. Good Samaritan (**Luke 10:25–37**), Jesus Calms the Storm (**Mark 4:36–41**), Conversion of St Paul (**Acts 9**).

When telling the **Christmas** and **Easter** events I often found it appropriate to just read the Bible narratives as they stand, or from the *Children's Story Bible* (Oxford, Lion, 1992).

Excerpts from these seasonal stories, presented in little booklets (often with illustrations) are available from Scripture Gift Mission, 3 Eccleston Street, London, SW1W 9LZ. I find these very useful to read and then leave for the children to look at. This organisation can also supply, for a donation, Scripture leaflets in numerous languages from all over the world, which are fun to look at and can be used in various ways in both assemblies and class activities.

11 SHOWING AND SHARING

These assemblies developed over the years into a vital part of our school life together, and although they occurred virtually every Friday morning, I have no notes about them at all. In essence, it began as an opportunity for children to bring into assembly some work, finished or not, that they wished to share with the school. Teachers suggested this to the pupils as well, naturally, and reminded them of the need to see me beforehand. But, as ever, we had to be flexible.

The usual procedure was for the child/children to see me during the week, ask me if they could show their item, let me know what they had to say and promise to practise this, in the hall if possible, so their voices were audible. It didn't always work out this way! If I could, I postponed some items, so we had a varied selection each week – writing of all sorts, topic folders, models, pictures, accounts of science experiments and investigative maths, reports of visits and sports fixtures, news from home and abroad, notices of weekend 'garage sales' for charity, a new pet, a trick to perform, an instrument to play ... on and on the list could go ... all were shared and celebrated.

Every child was named and thanked by me, or whoever was orchestrating the assembly.

Some weeks we had little, some too much, and keeping it lively and interesting wasn't always easy. But we persevered, made little rules and adjustments as we went along and enjoyed these times. We did sometimes spontaneously clap a child or group, or over one period of time, clap everyone at the end. Some schools have a **'clap-assembly'** in which this is the aim, to reinforce each child's success. If we had done this as a custom for each and every child separately we could have been there for hours! But the aim and intention is the same.

Another useful activity at these assemblies, time permitting, was for staff and children to ask questions of those presenting working models or describing their visit etc. This was done in a very relaxed, caring fashion, and had to be handled judiciously by the 'chairperson', but it provided another dimension in which we could learn. The speakers tried to explain how they did something, or problems they faced for instance, and the audience had to be patient as we explored new avenues together without prior notice.

Quite often in our sharing assemblies quieter children spoke about something that interested or concerned them for the very first time, or other surprises caught us all on the wrong foot! I find specific examples difficult to recall, so you are saved from any rambling details, suffice to say, we all considered these times valuable. I became a more tolerant and aware person through them, for a start. This didn't mean children were only able to 'speak' on Fridays. They were also encouraged to bring items before the school at any assembly, but usually by prior arrangement. Many groups, for example, worked for charities and arranged playtime and lunchtime events, entirely of their own volition. These were announced in assembly.

A list of dates and the teachers taking assembly was kept in the hall, along with the OHP transparencies, and children would then consult the member of staff (or me, if the list was missing!). Once systems are set up, they can become freer, and we managed very much like a large family to fit everything in.

As well, for a variation, we tried asking children to simply share an achievement with us. This proved a little more difficult to start with, and we left the idea 'on the back burner', from time to time, to avoid repetitions. Most children were content to do this from where they sat, or to be heard better, stand and move to a spot where they could see everybody. Some came to the front, if they preferred. This does enable more 'intangible' successes or those with no 'evidence' to hand to be celebrated.

Such valuable news as 'I never lost my temper once this week', or 'I enjoyed reading my book with Mrs. Brown' or 'I nearly swam a width yesterday, and next week I will!' Is worth sharing with a larger audience. It encourages every one, and gets you thinking about the successes regularly, even if they are not expressed out loud.

12 AN EXPERIENCE RECOUNTED

By this I mean an anecdotal account by a teacher of a personal experience. These were *very* personal at times, and it was good to see how honest and vulnerable colleagues were prepared to become with the children. Many of these stories were very powerful in helping us all to think, and think again about life and its meaning. Although there were less of them, these were the type of assemblies that were most likely to move children to write, respond and express opinions and even take action jointly to achieve a goal.

Often, other assemblies had this ingredient within them. Links with other sections of this book will be obvious to you. I have listed just a few. Some were too unusual to anticipate a helpful connection with a far-flung audience and others shared similarities that would make them unnecessary to mention. I sincerely hope that the fact that teachers did this, of their own choice, stimulates you to do the same. Whatever your choice of experience, enjoy preparing and re-telling it and may it bear fruit in the lives of the children.

- Sharing a surprise or a 'simple wonder' in life.
- Getting to know people at a barbecue or Family Wedding . . . analyse how it is done!
- Share a skill in detail, e.g. making a good white sauce, including preparation and washing-up.
- The day we had unexpected guests – how we felt and how we coped.
- A visit to a special school and the joy on the faces of those with cerebral palsy when they succeeded in manoeuvring their own wheelchairs – wow!
- Something interesting I did this weekend that helped our community (without bragging, many teachers reported in this vein on a Monday).
- Problems with my family and how we solved them, (very brave, and very encouraging).
- Visiting our friend in hospital; what we learnt and must remember, about health and caring for others.
- Remembering some old school friends and what we went through together. Happy memories and regrets – we all have them.
- My first attempt to use a microwave/ride a bike/play Nintendo – whatever. (We all make mistakes when learning!)
- Things I enjoy doing and why, e.g. collecting old clocks, cycling.
- Taking the youthclub for a night-time walk. The responsibility and fun ... stopping to hear the nightingale (only those who stood, quietly and still and tried to listen did so). Such tales could be linked with Matthew 7:24–27, Wise and Foolish Builders.
- When I got caught in a downpour. The initial panic and exasperation described, then enjoying it. To reinforce this optimism the teacher sang Burt Bacharach's *Raindrops Keep Fallin' On My Head*, holding an umbrella with cardboard water droplets hanging round it, labelled from drizzle, through shower, to downpour. Teachers, then children, all joined in. (Song 58 in *Allelujah!*, A&C Black.)
- Given a poster of an old farmer asleep on his haycart as the horse and dog alongside plod homeward, the teacher explained how he was seeking to live out the motto 'pursue gentleness' (1 Tim 6:11) . . . putting more effort into slowing down, caring and listening . . .

13 SOMEONE'S LIFE STORY

The list that follows is not especially startling, except to show the range of people we considered and what can be brought to the children's attention.

Often you will be able to bring **pictures, newspaper cuttings or artefacts** to illustrate your talk.

You will have to keep it within a 10/15 minute parameter, so don't get too detailed. As with Bible stories, it is far better to prepare and be able to tell the life story in your own way.

Perhaps you would like an older child to look-up the main facts for you, or find which books in your school library will be of help.

With all these, and many other people, their enthusiasm for life is abundantly obvious, so make sure the potted history reflects that.

There are news items or topical debates at times that will instigate an interest in the life history of a certain person. Use the opportunity.

Always link the past with present day realities, so the children can appreciate what was achieved and how it affects them.

Life stories

Henri Dunant (Red Cross)
Mother Theresa
Johnny Appleseed (try Reeve Lindbergh's poem, Joy Street Books)
St Francis of Assisi
Grace Darling
Guy Fawkes
Dr. Barnardo
George Muller
Lord Shaftesbury
William Wilberforce
John Newton
Nelson Mandela
Martin Luthe
Dr. Martin Luther King
Gladys Aylward
Amy Johnston
Wolfgang Mozart
Mahatma Ghandi
The Pilgrim Fathers (generalities)
Kunta Kinte (from *Roots* by Alex Hayley, London, Hutchinson, 1977)
Oliver Cromwell

14 USING PUPPETS

This is not easy to do well. It is a very powerful method, but takes a lot of practice. It has to be convincing enough to grab the children's attention and yet not be a 'show'.

I have used a hand-puppet and a marionette on strings. The former can be brought from a box, bag or basket or from a hidden space behind you, using a screen for example, as you sit or stand. The string puppet has to walk on to a table or platform, where you can easily operate it. It is best if it appears from behind some sort of screen too, rather than just 'materialise'. I have only tried, or seen used, one puppet at a time. The aim is to introduce a real character, to whom the children can relate.

Both the movements and voice will need to be very well rehearsed, so everything goes smoothly. When addressing or listening to the puppet you must be very involved and convincing. Although, with the hand puppets the purpose was for the children to really sympathise with him/her in the given situation, and the puppet character only communicated through the teacher, who was the trusted adult, in effect. So the voice, if you take this approach, is non-existent.

Two example assemblies to give a taste of the possibilities here:

a) Stand at a table and welcome everyone as usual. A strange guttural noise interrupts you (mouth doesn't move!) You look perplexed, try to continue, but it happens again ... you look for the answer, ask the children for help – then the gangly goo-ga bird (wooden string puppet with not many controls) appears slowly on the table. It introduces itself – you have to interpret for the school! – and say why it has come. You gladly give it time to 'speak' briefly and waddle off. It may bring something with it, like a piece of paper or a picture. I made the mistake of calling this creature he/him the first time and received complaints. So, as it is a weird bird, it was better all round to refer to **it**.
This creature came to tell us of environmental concerns/issues, or give a pat on the back for keeping the place tidy etc. It was a sort of 'green conscience', I suppose.

b) Sitting at the table, with breakfast laid, the teacher says 'Suzy will be arriving soon'. She is a black/white cuddly glove puppet. She glides in and starts to eat the cornflakes, then stops. You say 'good morning', puppet nods, and ask why she is not eating. Puppet lowers head and it is clear something is wrong.
You ask 'what's up?' No reply. She spills the cornflakes and keeps making excuses that the children can see the answers to, e.g. 'I can't find my book-bag' – when it is there for all to see. The children laugh and understand.
'Come on, let me know what's the matter . . . How can I help you if you don't tell me?'
Puppet slowly perks up, comes towards you and whispers in your ear.
'Oh, I see, it's something at school' (you repeat, as if children weren't there) . . . 'mmmm, oh, I see . . . someone is being unkind to you . . . well, you eat up your cornflakes and I will come to school with you and we'll talk with your teacher, OK?' Suzy nods, and gets back

Using Puppets

to eating.

You tell children, 'Suzy went to school, and we talked together with Mrs Claxton, her teacher.'

When Suzy came home . . . puppet re-emerges and you enact short scene in which Suzy tells how everything was sorted out and she had had a good day!

Suzy here is a part of the story-telling teacher's home only temporarily and doesn't have to do what is suggested!

The characters you invent (in quite some detail too) will need a convincing background and raison d'être, in order to keep coming to assembly for a purpose that fits the basic situation – as in the two examples given. Be brave, it's a winner! But, as with everything else that is like rich food, not too often. The relationship between you and the puppet can be developed as you proceed each time.

Having tried this approach and if you really want to go to town and invest in a larger puppet of your own, contact –

Children Worldwide
'Dalesdown'
Honeybridge Lane
Dial Post
Horsham
W. Sussex RH13 8NX
Tel: 01403 710712

They have a wide selection of all types of puppets, handmade to order (from around £30).

15 FURTHER SUGGESTIONS (INCLUDING PRAYER)

When considering assembly, be on the look out constantly – **newspaper headlines** may give a starting point. Watch the **television programmes** the children regularly view – at random times, to keep in touch.

Have you thought of inviting the local OAP club(s) or a class from a nearby special school to come and enjoy an assembly with you? A regular link in this way is good for everyone.

Ring the changes for those fixed festivals so things don't get stale –

Christmas 1. Investigate and celebrate customs round the world.
2. Use one carol's theme to think about in detail and make pictures for the hall.
3. Read the poem 'Christmas Star', Boris Pasternak in *Poems for Christmas* compiled by Zenka and Ian Coleman (London, Beaver Books, 1984) p 34 or the story 'Caspar and the Star', Francesca Bosca (Oxford, Lion, 1991).

Easter 1. Hold a painted egg display/competition for all who wish to enter.
2. 'Signs of new life' – start early to look for and wonder at nature's re-birth. Grow some bulbs in the hall for the whole school to watch.
3. Consider DEATH. A reality for all the natural world, plants, animals and humans (cf. *Emma Says Goodbye*, Carolyn Nystrom, Oxford, Lion, 1990).

Harvest 1. Celebrate the harvest of the sea, or the harvest of the woods and hedgerows.
2. Hold a packet only festival, where the whole display of gifts is only dry goods like sugar, lentils, cornflakes, rice etc. Discover where the products come from, and later (there is clearly no rush as nothing is perishable) decide together to whom you will send them.
3. Focus on a specific problem in one country, e.g. 'Mrs Mgamba's Hoe' – a true story from Zimbabwe. The hoes available were not strong enough to till the hard ground, so a new one was needed. The solution was simple, yet revolutionised local agriculture. New skills were re-introduced that colonialism had destroyed. Go on to do something to support the people there.
(Source – 'Intermediate Technology', see Appendix B.)

Compiling Acrostics is a thought-provoking task for each of these festivals/seasons as well. They can then be shared together in assembly.

Try a **school motto/slogan** for the week or month. New Year's resolutions mainly fade away, so a limited time-span is more rewarding. Children or staff can suggest some that can be discussed, and voted on. This is an excellent exercise in collaborative decision making and is non-threatening for everyone. Teachers can lead by example in this situation. To start you off, how about:

'Lend a hand, give a smile.'
'It's pick-up litter week.'

Further Suggestions

'We all stand together' (McCartney song).

Have a brief report from different classes each day during the week to gauge success. More suitable for Juniors, but adaptable for infant children. The long term aim is to make these attitudes an integral part of everyday life.

Whilst on the subject of collaboration, why not take an assembly or two in **partnership** with another teacher? Discussing the presentation together will without doubt help to give you insights and ideas. It also provides you with two voices and faces to use, so a conversational piece is very applicable here. It is helpful to involve all the teachers directly from time to time as well. Perhaps by giving each one a card to read out in response to a question, or asking those prepared to do so to respond 'off the cuff' to a suggestion or request. Teachers (and other staff) really working together are a good example for the children, who do notice these things!

Watch the school grounds and use them as a stimulus. So many children pass by beautiful things everyday and don't notice them. Bring in some home-grown leaves in autumn, or a teasel head. Give every child a sunflower seed to plant and care for – somewhere! Ask for volunteers to draw a sketch or plan of the school environment in their own way.

Practise your expressions of surprise/inquisitiveness/joy etc. in front of the mirror! Yes, theatrical, but very important. Your facial expression during assembly is a great asset to ensure control and involvement.

Try something DIFFERENT!

When children are used to behaving sensibly, a small risk is not disruptive. Link the start with the theme, naturally, but how about –

- Walking in backwards (direction/progress)
- Appearing suddenly from behind a board (surprises, feelings)
- Sitting in your usual place and apparently forgetting it's your turn (memory, feelings)
- Hitting a shuttle cock high up in the air and asking children to watch its descent (observation, flight). Perhaps the child who catches it can be asked to do something in the assembly.
- It's also extremely good for the children, when ready, to fully 'chair' proceedings in some assemblies.
- Children do respond to each other, and another nice start is to have a few children at the front doing something intently in silence, oblivious to everyone arriving, e.g. checking bicycle, painting a large picture or doing an experiment.

And finally to the vexed subject of prayer

I agree with Ofsted! In guidance to Inspectors it was stated categorically that 'Worship is generally understood to imply the recognition of a supreme being'.[1] How can you recognise someone by pretending he/she isn't there? I think appropriate short prayers are quite acceptable in school assembly, but then you know that already, if you have read through this book.

Prefaced with something like, 'I will say this prayer and hope you can make the words your own' OR 'This is a prayer so-and-so used at such-and-such a time that may help us' OR 'Say Amen at the end if you wish', to enable children to join in as they decide, prayers can be meaningful and effective.

Special Times

Just the same as a time of contemplative silence can become devalued, if always used in assembly, vary your approach to prayer too. Spontaneous prayer is part of reality too for any faith. When a catastrophe such as a typhoon strikes a country, for those who believe in God, a prayer on behalf of these people is essential, surely? The eloquence of no prayer, from a known believer, can be as devastating as the tragic event itself to children learning about moral and spiritual values, in a confusing and suffering world.

Sometimes we said an old school prayer together –

> 'Dear Lord, please bless our school,
> that working together and playing together
> we may learn to serve you and serve one another'

During a project on Victorian Days, it may well be pertinent to look at some nineteenth-century prayers on the OHP, and note their simplicity and sincerity.

Phrasing your own prayers is much to be preferred, but a helpful book that has a great variety is *The Lion Book of Children's Prayers* by Mary Bachelor. If you wish to think about the topic of prayer with the school, two publications I found very helpful are:

Your kingdom come – praying for the poor. An international application of each section of the Lord's prayer published by Tear Fund. (See Appendix B for address.)

Roy Mitchell's *Book of Cartoons* 'God is . . .' (London, Harper Collins, 1990), which has several applicable to prayer, such as:

GOD IS: Longing to hear from you
   not deaf
   never too busy to listen
   not impressed by waffle.

I acquired permission from the publishers to use up to six of these cartoons on OHP transparencies in school only. They are humorous and readily understood. Maybe if more primary schools request this facility, the best of the book will be turned into transparencies by the author!

Children can also be asked, of course, to write their own prayers, and be encouraged to respond in this way if they so decide, when happy, puzzling or sad news is shared. The more honest they are, the better.

1. Ninth issue of an Ofsted In-house publication 'Update' (Sept 1994).

16 PROVOCATIVE PICTURES

Fifteen OHP transparencies, chosen for impact as discussion starters in assembly, and/or to lead to wider themes. Some opening questions are given here.
Suggested Themes:

1. '**Money**, money, money'. Use ABBA song, 'The love of money is the root of all kinds of evil' (1 Timothy 6:10).
    How do you react to this picture?
    What are 'values' in life? Is money in the bank a reliable security?

2. 'A foot in each camp', or haltering between two opinions!
    How long before he has to make his mind up? What does this tell us about life's **decisions?**
    Jesus said 'You cannot serve two masters.'(Matthew 6:24)

3. 'Unto us a **son** is given' the promise of the prophet Isaiah, fulfilled in Jesus.
    A promise for all people, of all nations.
    What does the picture tell us?

4. **Co-operation** – imagine the conversation between the two donkeys (see Assembly No. 2).

5. 'I took 5 steps today' – why is she so excited?
    What can we **achieve** today?
    What are our attitudes to the difficulties of life?

6. Faces tell a story (see Assembly 5). A person cries/laughs. What do you think is going on here in the life of each person? Explain your ideas. The pictures are from Romania, the Philippines, India, Rwanda. Think of people's varied **needs** and how they change.

7. Football fans – What's the problem here?!
    What does this tell us about people?
    Why can't they watch the game together in **safety**?

8. What are all the animals up to, and why?
    Is there a germ of truth in the picture?
    Explain together.
    What are we doing to our **environment**/surroundings?

9. An African boy eats – what is unusual about this, do you think? He is lonely, orphaned and someone has to **care** for him. How does this affect me/us?

Special Times

10. **Patterns** – these can be enjoyed for their beauty and precision, in the first place. How wonderful that a person can design things like this. Yet, they were generated by computer to help explain 'chaos theory' . . . all very complicated.
    Search for patterns around the school . . . in creation . . .

11. **A shanty town** in Peru. Look carefully and see how other people live, often despite working hard. Why, do you think, are they so poor? Compare their homes to yours. Encourage the children to be grateful for what they have and enjoy and, perhaps, do something to help the poor.

12. Fleeing **refugees** . . . another few thousand people have to leave their homes. Why does this happen? Life so often, isn't at all fair. These people are, in fact, Kurds fleeing from Iraq. Remember, Joseph and Mary took Jesus to Egypt. Refugees lose homes, family, friends, security and often their sense of purpose.

13. The road to school – usually safe and secure. What has happened to this town? A photo from a town in **Bosnia** to talk about.

14. Two **Harvest** stories – success in Kabul, Afghanistan and Nepal. What is common to these two stories?
    Ahmed was working on a water improvement scheme and being paid in grain. Paying wages in inflation-proof food supported the efforts to rebuild a city devastated by war. One sack was two weeks' wages.
    Lila was trained to help farmers make better use of their hillside fields. Soil is easily washed away and the right choice of crop is important. Everyone has to grow their own food.

15. The **osprey** – here's one fishing! He was seen in Scotland, but seven young ones were moved to Rutland Water in 1996. They are fitted with identity rings and radio transmitters and the hope is they will nest and colonise in England. Why is this important do you think?
    A colour brochure on the osprey project is available from Anglian Water Birdwatching Centre, Rutland Water Nature Reserve, Egleton, Oakham LE15 8BT (01572 770651).

17 INTRODUCING THE WORKED EXAMPLES OF ASSEMBLIES

Now for something slightly different, for those who like an assembly, or two, ready to hand, but adaptable. There follows a series of 18 suggestions that can be photocopied and used as an aide-memoire in assembly. The guidance given is somewhat fuller and the material could be expanded to cover several assemblies (pass the sheet on to another teacher).

Space is left for your own pencil notes, which are important. This space can also be used as a record of how and when the theme was used and other ideas developed later.

These sample scripted assemblies can be used quickly. Each will last about 15 minutes. Items that need some preparation are highlighted in the text in bold type. It is not possible to give exact words for you to say when the children have been asked to do or say something themselves. Your response depends on theirs, and you must therefore act accordingly or perhaps deviate from the script!

You may, of course, need to repeat a question, or comment, or slightly re-phrase it for the children to grasp. Be aware, keep the children involved.

Assemblies

Assembly 1: *The Wonder of Colour*

INTRODUCE the theme by having a **black and white television**, in front of the children, turn it on (keeping the volume low) as they come into the hall and sit attentively before it yourself. (Sit sideways on to the children so that you can give an eye and ear to them too!)

Simulate enwrapped involvement with the screen. There will probably be a few restless stirrings, but never mind – few children see a b/w television these days. Most will stare with you. Turn round and ask, 'What is missing then?'

You may get other suggestions, but accept them with thanks, and having got the answer colour or colours, turn off the TV.

Reiterate, 'Yes, the colour is missing, the picture is only black and white. Early television sets were like this.

'Just suppose our world was really like those pictures on the screen, only black and white and grey ... no colour at all ... or like this **display**.

Move in, or uncover slowly, whichever is easier, a free standing display of black and white newspaper sheets, including some pictures. These are necessary now to focus the children's attention, as you speak.

'Think of a world like this, all the time! (Point to display and pause). Look around our hall at the colours we can see and enjoy.' Pick out some examples, as appropriate, e.g. 'the balls for PE are red, blue, green, yellow, the floor tiles are spotted white and brown, the doors are painted ... wonderful!'

What if all around us was like this board here (point to it, stare at it) just black and white? . . . .Some children may want to respond at this point. Take the opportunity to listen together to their answers. You don't need to comment, other than be enthusiastic to accept the ideas with a 'yes' and a smile.

'I am going to read to you a story about a world that was just black and white.'

Read the **book** *The Day it Rained in Colours* by Roy E Merton (Oxford, Lion, 1973). It may be best to read the first eight pages, then summarise briefly in your own words how the children tried to rectify things then read what happened when the Maker is asked to help. (Last 12 pages.)

At the end pause and ask 'How did the people in the story react to the changes in their world?' Take a few answers, not too many, and summarise in the children's own words.

It will be something like – 'Yes, that's it, they were really happy, amazed and delighted. So, how should we feel about a world that is always full of colour? The same way, yes.' Repeat the descriptions given by your children of their feelings.

'Let's be still for a moment, close your eyes, and think of your favourite colour. Think of all the lovely colours in our school, the colours of the flowers and our clothes. Say your own quiet thank you prayer for the wonder of colour!'

A few moments of quietness.

Now let's sing 'I can sing a rainbow' (p 5 in *Apusskidu*, A&C Black) or 'Many shades of blue' (published in Infant projects No. 64, Warwick, Scholastic, 1969) words and music by Christopher Williams. Or a similar song.

Notes

Further ideas for assembly and class activities

1. Make a collection of objects of only one colour. The variety of shades can be pointed out, and this can be linked with the fact that even when it's gloomy and cloudy, we can still see and enjoy colours as they change slightly.

2. Collect and display a range of **patterns** and **pictures**, some in colour, some with restricted colour, some in black and white. Talk together about the positive qualities of each group.

3. Read the poem 'Crayoning' by Stanley Cook from *A Very First Poetry Book* ed. John Foster (Oxford, OUP, 1984) p 14. Ask two children to paint the picture as you read each item of the house. (**A big white board and paint and brushes** will have to be ready.) Ask the school/class to explain what is actually happening as each word is read (e.g. the blue door). The painters are choosing the colour by its name/their experience and using it accordingly. Stress again the wonder of colours, that we can see and recognise each one.

4. Use tissue paper to make some patterns, through which a torch or projector light can be shone, to accentuate and 'brighten' the colours for all to see and enjoy.

5. Read poems 'Mixing Colours' (Eric Finney) and 'I Like Colours' (Pie Corbett) from the first pages of *A Red Poetry Paintbox* (Oxford, OUP, 1994).
6. See also Assembly 15: The Rainbow.

Notes

Assembly 2: *Co-operation*

Put the **OHP transparency of the two donkeys (No 4)** up on the screen/wall for the children to see and think about as they come into assembly.

Once everyone is settled, cover with a piece of plain paper all the pictures except the first and ask 'What is happening here?'

The children will explain the problem in their own ways. Summarise their opinions and then in a similar way, go through each picture, asking questions like:

2. 'What happened next?'
3. 'Did this help either of them? Why not?'
4. 'What do you think they are doing now?'
5. 'What did they decide together?'
6. So, the next step was to . . . ?.

'Now, look at the words above and below the pictures – co-operation is better than conflict.' (If appropriate ask the children to say the words again with you.)

'How was this true for the two donkeys?' Work at the answers until you are sure a clear explanation has been given in various ways. (Take off OHP transparency and have a **blank acetate** ready to write on.)

'Yes, they couldn't feed whilst they were struggling against each other, but if they went together to each pile and ate their share, both of them were happy.' How did this come about? . . . yes, by discussion (yes, our donkeys can talk!) stopping and working out the problem together. TOGETHER – that is the important word in solving problems, disagreement or conflict.'

'Both of the donkeys had an equal right to eat, but they also had an equal responsibility to help each other.'

'What conflicts/problems can you think of that arise between children in school?' . . . get a few suggestions and then choose one to refer to, e.g. a child has been promised by some friends that she/he can play in a game, but all the spaces have been taken up.

'When faced with difficult conflicts like this we often get UPSET – (write word on OHP)

'So like the donkey, STOP (add word below)

'and BE CALM (add words below)

'and THINK TOGETHER (add words below)

Join up with arrows as you repeat

'This means talking about the conflict listening to other points of view, so together a solution is found.'

⇨ UPSET?
⇩
STOP
⇩
BE CALM
⇩
THINK TOGETHER

'If the children in our example did that, what sort of solutions/ideas might they come up with, when a game is full-up and a promise needs to be kept?'

As the children express their ideas, ask someone else to repeat one or two of them to emphasise the necessity to listen to each other.

'Remember, when trying to find a solution it is important to discover how the other person feels, as well as yourself.'

'Put up your hand if you have been in a disagreement or conflict with other children recently.'

Summarise the position, e.g. 'I see, about half of you.'

'Think of the donkeys and how working together helped them. Put up your hand if you want to try and remember and use our plan to solve your problems (point to words on OHP one by one and then turn machine off) and use it next time . . . good, a lot of you will . . . GREAT.'

'Remember the donkeys . . . remember too, problems are inevitable, violence is optional and it solves nothing. WORK TOGETHER!'

Finish by singing 'I get by with a little help from my friends' (song 38, *Allelujah!* A&C Black).

Further ideas for assembly and class activities

1. Read through together and discuss the 'Resolution Rap' (see Appendix D). Have fun!

2. Use the photocopiable 'All about me' sheet (see Appendix D) .Each child can write and or draw about him/herself and create a T-shirt that shows how unique and special they are. These can be displayed or shared within the school assembly or class, as considered helpful, with the aim of recognising and tolerating differences between people.

3. Read the Jungle Doctor fable of the competition to win a melon (p 34 in *Jungle Doctor's Hippo Happenings,* Paul White, Exeter, Paternoster Press, 1966). Ask , 'Why did the giraffes win so easily?'

4. Play the tape of Paul McCartney's song, 'We all pull together' (from animated featurette *Rupert and the Frog Song,* HPL publications. Music sheet MY 70549, Communications Music Sales Ltd., 78 Newman Street, London W1P 3LA).

5. Collect photos and pictures of teamwork of all types that can be displayed and profitably discussed.

6. Refer to the Bible verse in Amos 3:3 . . . 'Do two walk together unless they agree to do so?' . . . agreeing an aim has to come first. This shared purpose comes about by talking/listening to each other. Explain too that adults – teachers, parents – have to do this.

7. List ways in which the children think they can work together and suggest they review how they are getting on each month. Encourage them to look out for differences of opinion and how they are resolved.

Assembly 3: *Getting Along Together*

'Good morning, once again. We are all here day by day, week by week. At school and at home, living with people closely around us is not always easy going.

'Perhaps even this morning something someone has said has upset you; or perhaps you have been unkind in what you have said . . . just think about this for a moment (a moment to pause) . . . have you?

'Listen to this **poem**' (read 'Truth' by Wade, from his anthology *Conkers*, Oxford, OUP, 1989, p 9).

'Words do matter . . . choose them carefully. As an old lady used to say to her children . . . "engage brain before opening mouth".

'Why do you think this is important?' (Take a few suggestions from children at this point. The exact words you use will be governed by their responses.)

'Look at this **block of wood**. I am now going to **hammer** in a **nail*** (do so a little way). Our unkind words are like this nail. Often said out of frustration/anger/impatience, we say things we ought not to. They hurt people, they hurt us.' They are forced into people's minds and hearts. (Bang a little more as you speak, synchronised to words.) 'Sometimes we say unkind words again . . . and again . . . and again.

'Look' (hold wood by nail) . . . 'the nail is firmly fixed.' (Try to pull the two apart, grimacing theatrically to make the point.)

'Words are remembered, they remain in people's minds and their effects are not easily removed.'

(With a pair of **pliers or pincers** hold up the wood and remove the nail, showing the effort needed.) 'The nail was hard to remove.'

'When we have said unkind words, it requires effort to put things right too . . . what would you suggest?' . . . (take some ideas).

'Yes, saying sorry that you were rude/nasty helps, so does sharing a kindness, because, look . . . here where the nail was is a mark. The nail has gone . . . but the dent remains.' (Show it all around.)

'Our unkind/hasty words are like that too . . . the hurt can remain for a while, it may take time to heal.

'When I fill in this hole, perhaps with Polyfilla, the filler will fit the hole exactly. In the same way our apologies and attempts to put things must fit precisely, suited to the person and the situation not a vague mumbled "sorry".

'So be thoughtful . . . look . . . I am now driving a **screw** into the wood, it's hard going.' (Pause to emphasise). 'Next I'll undo it (do so) and try again with a little **soap** rubbed on the screw' (put some on).

'It's much easier now to do the job. Kind words, helpful words, are like the soap – they make life easier.' (Drive in the screw, with your **screwdriver**.)

'What sort of words will make life smoother/easier for us, as we live together, work together?' (Take a few suggestions)

'It isn't easy to use these words to show kindness. We need help, so let's ask God to help us, to make the effort.'

Sing – 'Cross over the road' (p 97, BBC *Come and Praise*)

*Note – it may help to prepare holes for the nails and screws beforehand!

Further ideas for assembly and class activities

1. List as many words as you can that help to make life easier
   e.g. Please
     Thank you
       May I?
       Excuse me

   and little things we can do

   e.g. smile
       wait your turn
       open the door

2. Read the poem again and discuss some of the thoughts more precisely, e.g. how can words be like 'ghosts' in your minds? Cuts and grazes do heal, don't they? How long does it take for you?

3. How do we make things run smoothly in a large community like our school? Exchange ideas and try some of them out. It's very helpful to have a time for reports of occasions when children's words have been thoughtful and encouraging to their peers.

4. Consider the strength of friendship. Read and discuss the ancient wisdom of Ecclesiastes 4 verses 9–12 and apply it to daily life today.

5. Ideas for getting along together can be shared in class 'Circle Time'.

Notes

Assembly 4: *Lost and Found*

As the children come into the assembly, have the words of the song 'Think of all the things we lose . . .'(song 57, *Come and Praise*, BBC) on the **OHP screen**.

Point to the words from time to time and gesture with your finger to your eyes and your temple to show that you want the children to look and think about the song.

Once everyone is in, sing the song together. At the end, keep the words up and continue – 'Let's consider what this song is saying, carefully, together this morning . . . it isn't only about things. We have a box in school that we use for lost property and so we know for sure about some of the things we lose, leave behind, forget day by day (mention and show particular items if you wish) Some things are big, some small, that get mislaid, as we say. This happens at home too, of course. Think about things you lose quite often . . . what are they?'

Take a few examples from the children (if you wish a list can be made, either by you on a board or a teacher/child with pen and paper for future use) looking for different items . . . 'That'll do for the present, we have 10 things, some repeated. Now, let's look at the list in the song . . . what's there?'

Have the children read one or two out loud e.g. pencil sharpeners, books, shoes . . . (turn off the OHP). 'Some matter more than others . . . that depends on us'

'These are all everyday bits and pieces, always in use. But three (or whatever number) of you mentioned PE and games kit . . . why are these items often "lost"? Why is it, do you think?' . . . (pause a moment, then take answers . . .)

What you want is a comment like – 'it's when we have to change in a hurry, then things get lost'.

'Yes, you see, when a lot is going on all at once and you are all changing, one set of clothes for another, and thinking about what you are going to do next . . . it's then that a sock or shoe can easily go missing . . . we are all so busy and perhaps excited. It is, at those times that we need extra care and to help each other.'

'When something is lost, five pairs of eyes are better than one . . . searching for the missing item, and oh, the relief when it is found! I wonder what you have lost and were very worried about? How did you feel when you found it, perhaps after lots of looking, perhaps by chance days later?

'Things are found again, fortunately, so we feel . . . ?' Get a few suggestions, so you can proceed to use the children's descriptions e.g. 'We all know the happy, thankful, relieved feeling of lost things being found.'

Turn on OHP and ask 'But what else does the song say, we lose and find?' . . . pause and take answers . . . 'Yes, it's our friendships.' You may get other ideas like nerves/opportunities/names/good feelings, but just say 'these we can think about another time, let's think about friends this time.' And return to the other ideas another day.

'How do we lose friends, do you think? Look again at the song words, especially verse three.' Point to OHP, and allow a little thinking time. Hands will go up, so get as many different ideas as you can, and then, having affirmed each one, summarise, e.g. . . . (turn off OHP)

Notes

'OK, so we have considered the song a bit more and think we can lose friends by unkind words, not sharing, impatience, not wanting to play with them, or listen to them, perhaps ignoring them because we are so busy, just like losing our tee shirts! . . . we always need to be aware of these situations. We don't want to lose good friends for ever.'

'So how can we "find" good friends again, do you think? You know, when you and a friend have perhaps argued and you miss each other.'. . . Take some answers quite quickly now as you draw to a close . . . 'Yes, that's it, by saying sorry, showing kindness or generosity, being considerate, going out of your way to help, and that all takes real effort, it won't always be easy.'

'Remember lost friendships, like lost pens, may have to be searched for, and that may take some time and energy on your part.'

'Let's now pause, close our eyes, think in the quietness about this . . . in your own mind, be thankful for lost friends found, . . . ask God to help you remake lost friendships, perhaps . . . Think of ways we can help each other in this . . . and learn about God, our special perfect Friend, together.'

Further ideas for assembly and class activities

1. Pursue the ideas left 'in the air', e.g. *lost* opportunities (the song can be used again for this, if you wish), time and freedoms. These are slightly different in nature, and may never be found again because circumstances change. Children often point this out themselves and older pupils may wish to discuss this more fully.

2. Read the parables of Luke 15 – The lost sheep (verses 1–7), the lost coin (verses 8–10) and the lost son (verses 11–24) – each illustrating our lostness in relation to God. The prodigal son shows the heart of a loving Father-God searching for his children. Use NIV, Contemporary English version or Good News Bible, or read from a good retold story, e.g. Timothy Dudley-Smith's *Stories of Jesus* (Oxford, Lion, 1986).

3. Hold a 'be positive' day to encourage children to seek out and take opportunities for positive helpful action, e.g. holding open a door for a visitor.

4. Read and talk about Michael Rosen's poem 'Losing things' p 104 of his anthology *Quick, Let's Get Out of Here* (London, Puffin, 1985).

5. Ask children to write about a time they felt 'lost' (lonely or bewildered) and see if they will share their feelings and thoughts with each other.

6. Use the list of lost items made in assembly and suggested by the children, not only to talk about how to look after things, but also widening the discussion to include precise ways in which we find/lose or make/remake friendships.

Assembly 5: *We All Have Feelings – Anger*

As a general introduction, use the **OHP transparency No 6: four faces**.

'Look at these four faces. How do you think each of these people is feeling?'

Look at the four in turn, quite quickly, agreeing together the type of look on each:

Top left – 'yes, he seems to look bewildered, lost, feeling sad and lonely, uncertain.'
Top right – 'she's really happy, contented, smiling broadly.'
Bottom left – 'she's happy too; a big smile, wide open eyes, beaming joyfully.'
Bottom right – 'a real contrast, head bowed, feeling sad, even despair.'

'We'll talk about where these people come from and why they are feeling the way they are another day (see further ideas) . . . but, all people have feelings . . . round the world people feel tired and happy, sad and excited, unsure and jealous . . . and so on.

'We feel different at different times . . . we are not always buoyantly happy, sometimes we are feeling guilty, other times worried. What we have to learn is to be honest about our feelings and learn to control them, not let them control us.

'Today let's think about a feeling that can be very strong – anger. Have any of you ever felt really angry? . . . (some children will admit to this readily, others are more reticent) . . . would someone tell us when they felt angry and why?' . . . allow time for thinking and take just two or three replies . . .

'So, you were angry and cross because someone had cheated in a game, or you were feeling tired and the music at home was so loud you couldn't go to sleep . . .' summarise like this what you have been told.

'Now for a story . . . *Angry Arthur*.' Read the **book** by Haiwin Oram (London, Red Fox, 1993). This is short, so go through slowly, showing appropriate pictures.

'If you feel angry then, don't *blow-up*, like Arthur (wave your arms in the air and pretend to be angry, scowling), that helps no one (smile at this point!), but don't *clam-up* either . . . this is sulking, being resentful and awkward (act this out too, mainly with your face, pouting). Both these reactions damage us and other people . . . be honest and ask why you are feeling angry.

'Is it because you are just   fed up and bored?
                                   want your own way?
                                   you're tired and irritable?

'Anger is often this selfish! Like Arthur's was. So face up to it, and keep your feelings under control . . . perhaps just keeping your mouth shut and counting to 10 slowly! . . . so the situation eases.'

'The Bible tells us – a fool gives full vent to his anger, but a wise man keeps himself under control (Prov 29:11).

'Yes, keeping control is very sensible, it helps everyone including you. Decide to be a builder not a destroyer, a help not a hindrance. Don't be an Arthur! Oh no!

'But there are times (certainly less common, it must be said) when we feel angry on behalf of someone else. It's a feeling that pushes us into action to do something good.'

'For example, Bob Geldorf, a pop singer, felt very angry some years ago when governments were just leaving millions to starve to death in Ethiopia. He organised Band Aid, a great concert to raise money to help send food, and this work continued for years and led to today's Red Nose charity days, which involve millions of people. It was a magnificent effort, spurred on by a feeling of anger.'

'So, if after thinking about it, you're sure your angry feeling is a right one, do something about it. Talk about it with a friend, or relative, find out what they think: you may be able to do something useful.

'Now let's talk to God,

> Lord, we thank you for our feelings. They tell us that we are alive. Help us to use them well and be aware of how others feel too.'

End with a favourite song, that makes you all feel good, perhaps chosen by a child.

Further ideas for assembly and class activities

1. The photos on the OHPT are from Romania/the Philippines/Rwanda and India (clockwise from top left). You can go on to recall this with the children and discuss the four situations – orphaned/living in a caring village/on the run from persecution/having received aid after a storm

2. Tell the children about 'FIRST AID' for that cross feeling, so we don't inflict damage –
   either a) count slowly to 10
      or b) think of a pleasant place
      or c) close your mouth tightly and breathe slowly through your nose
      or all three . . .
   These exercises simply help us to stop, get control and think, but they're fun to talk about! Then the problem needs to be attended to (see Assembly 2 'Co-operation').

3. There are poems worth reading and discussing, e.g. 'Grudges', Ruth Nichols, *Another Second Poetry Book* (Oxford, OUP, 1988) p 71. 'Bored', John Kitching, *Me and You and Poems 2*, ed. Rolf Harris, (Knight, 1993) p 44. 'The Quarrel', Mike Winyard, *Wheel Around the World* (Macdonald, 1983) p 22. 'What, Me?', Brian Morse, *Plenty of Time* (London, Bodley Head, 1994) p 51. 'Music', Tony Mitton, a poem about good feelings, *Purple Poetry Paintbox* (Oxford, OUP, 1996) p 48.

4. Proceed to deal with other feelings and the power they generate, e.g. embarrassment, which can be tackled with humour. Describe the warm glow/wanting to hide oneself in a hole feeling! Being honest with the children about how *you* feel in given situations is a good starting point. Everyone then realises that we all do have feelings and can support one another in controlling them.

5. A series of 10 books called 'Feelings', by Janine Amos (Bath, Cherry Tree Books, 1993), is well worth referring to. They encourage talk through short stories and questions, and cover – Afraid, Angry, Brave, Confident, Friendly, Happy, Hurt, Jealous, Lonely and Sad.

6. How we feel in certain situations can be discussed in 'Circle Time'.

Notes

Assembly 6: *Channels*

'These words are based on the well-known prayer of St Francis of Assisi:

> 'Make me a channel of your peace,
> where there is hatred, let me bring your love,
> where there is injury, pardon,
> where there is despair, hope,
> where there is darkness, light,
> where there is sadness, joy,
> O Master, grant that I may not seek to be consoled,
> so much as to console,
> to be understood, as to understand,
> to be loved, as to love with all my soul.'

Now you will need – **a plant in a pot**, some **guttering or drainpipe** (about ½m), **a jug of water.**

Place one end of the guttering (to be preferred because you can see what's happening) on the end of the table, with the other end leading into the plant pot.

You can set this up in front of the children, but practise first, however simple it may seem. As you do, speak to gain their attention:

'Well done, you listened carefully to those famous words and later we will sing them. First, though, I have something to do . . . so, we'll put the plant down here on this box . . . then lower this bit of guttering left over from our extension, so it runs from the table . . . right, now here (show them, hold it high) I have a jug of water . . . what do you think I'm going to do next?' . . .

Only one answer will probably be needed! 'Yes, pour the water into the guttering/pipe . . . so what will happen?' Take an answer or two, keep things moving. 'Good, yes, the water runs down the guttering, flowing nicely . . . (pour just a little) and the plant is nicely watered, the soil is now damp.

'Let's just think about this, for a moment, and link it with our song.'

'The guttering is acting as a channel, guiding the water from here (point to top) down to the plant (point clearly again) . . . St Francis' prayer asked that he (not other people – but he himself) would be like a channel, that peace, love, pardon and so on would flow through him. He wanted God to make him useful. St Francis was not the source of this peace, anymore than the guttering is the water. They are separate. He wants to be the means of passing on love and harmony – touching and refreshing the lives of others. Just as the water reaches the plant with the help of this guttering.

'Are we like St Francis I wonder? Wanting to be as helpful each day? If so, where does all the hope/love/peace come from?' . . . have a pause to take answers, which will give you a clear indication of what else to deal with in other assemblies and/or help you to continue . . . 'Right, God gives such things to us. He is the source of all goodness. Remember, Jesus said to his disciples, "My peace, I give it you . . ." that's just one example (from John 14:27).

'That's why Francis was asking God to make him a channel of God's peace, we too can pray, make me a channel of your peace.

'So, let's do that together. We'll sing the song based on St Francis'

Notes

words (No 43 in *Allelujah!*, A&C Black and 147 in *Come and Praise 2*, BBC) If you believe there is another source of peace and joy, then use it and pass the blessing on.'

If the words are on the OHP, you could alternatively read them together, slowly.

'To finish, I think the plant needs another little watering, so who would like to come and pour a little more water down our channel here?' (point) . . .

Choose a sensible volunteer, and thank him/her after the job is done.

'Good, let's all be as keen ourselves to be *channels* of good things, like peace and joy.'

Further ideas for assembly and class activities

1. Give a short life history of St Francis, whose deeds were as important as his words and are still influential today, hundreds of years on. It may be preferred to ask the children first to find out more about him.

2. With the same equipment repeat the illustration, but then use some clothes or plastic to block the guttering. Explain that the water is still the same, but the plant sits and waits, receiving nothing, getting drier. Discuss with the children, why this is so, how the water is prevented from flowing down. Ask the children to apply this to everyday living, what sort of things block the flow/stop us being channels?

3. Give a personal word about the challenge that this illustration brings to you.

4. 'If we are like the guttering, what are we passing on to others day by day, at school and at home?' Ask the children to consider at the end of the day both the good and the bad influences they have had on each other. Perhaps some would like to disagree with the whole illustration! Don't be afraid to take opposing viewpoints.

5. Look again at the prayer, choose three salient words and apply these in practical, helpful terms, e.g.
    our attitudes to each other
    offering help
    being patient
    going to the end of the queue.

6. Gifts are things that are given, freely. Look together at the wide world and consider other gifts we are given to share, e.g.
    laughing
    the countryside
    encouragement
    knowledge.

7. Another song to sing 'Peace, perfect peace is the gift of Christ, our Lord' (song No. 53 *Come and Praise* BBC, London, 1978).

Assembly 7: *Darkness and Light*

Introduction – Give an example from your own experience when you have been moving around in a place familiar to you, but in the dark. A family occasion is even better where several people are trying to find their way, some less confident than others.

e.g. 'Last week our family got home a bit late from a day out. We parked our motor caravan in the usual spot on the drive, beside the garage, but because we were late, we got out down the steps at the back out into the darkness'.

'The street lights don't help in our back garden, so we stopped for a moment to get used to the gloom. The children, who are about the same age as you, groped along the hedge to find the gap through into the garden.

' "I think it's here somewhere," says one . . . "Just a bit further," another comments, pushing a little. . . . "Take it easy, I can't see where I am going," is the reply.' (Try to act this out a bit as you speak.) . . . 'At last we file through . . . before us is the garden, where the children are used to playing.

'But they are hesitant . . . exactly where is the sandpit with a low wall around it? They laugh as one of them walks into the edge of the flower bed round the shed! The youngest starts to cry, "I'm scared, Daddy . . ." "Hold my hand," says her older sister . . . "What's that strange thing there?" . . . "It's only the shadow of the bush across the bumpy path" . . . "It looks really weird . . ."

'I wonder if you have experienced something like that?' (You may get some nods or 'yes, I haves', so pause to listen to one or two accounts if the children wish to share.) 'Maybe indoors, maybe outside . . . things look different, and distances are hard to judge. That night in our garden everything was the same as we had left it in the morning – the trees hadn't moved, the shed hadn't swapped places with the sandpit' (smiles all round) ' . . . but we couldn't see clearly, in the gloom shapes looked unusual and making progress was slow and difficult. We got back safely to the back door in the end though!

'Sometimes, there are strange sounds that disturb us too, like owls hooting or foliage rustling . . .

'What would have helped us in this situation, do you think?' Pause, take a few suggestions from the children.

'Yes, some sort of light . . . as it happened we had a torch in the van, but the batteries were flat! . . . A torch would certainly have helped us to see the way ahead, like this.'

Produce a **torch**. If you can effectively black out the hall beforehand, now turn off the lights and shine the torch in various directions.

'Look at the beam of light, it penetrates the darkness, showing us things clearly . . . If I turn it off and on (do so several times) you can see this for yourself . . . off . . . and on, the light pushes through the darkness . . .

'Darkness, is an absence of light . . . we all find parts of life dark and hard, so some light to show us what is real, to help us see the way is of great value.

'God's word, the Bible is described as "A lamp to our feet and a light for our path" (Ps 119:105) . . . showing us the way through life, revealing what we can't see or aren't sure of, removing worries and so on.'

Notes

Hold up a copy of the **Bible or New Testament** . . . and simply comment, 'It's well worth reading, an effective light . . . a guide to living.

'Now let's sing the first two verses of our song. "And God said . . . (See p.88 Appendix E.)

Further ideas for assembly and class activities

1. Read and talk about a poem on the theme – e.g. 'Shadow man', John Foster, *Oxford Blue Poetry Paintbox* (Oxford, OUP, 1994) p 22.
'Things which go bump', Andrew Collett, *Purple Poetry Paintbox* (Oxford, OUP, 1996) p 4.
'In the dark', Jane Pridemore, *Poetry Plus*, Book 4. Green earth and silver stars. (Schofield and Simms, 1982) p 19.
'The house at night', James Kirkup, *Another Third Poetry Book* (Oxford, OUP, 1988) p 64.

2. Perhaps the children would like to write and draw about their own experiences. 'In the dark.'

3. Jesus said – 'I am the light of the world' (John 8:12). There is also a promise that follows. Explain in your own words how this works in your life or the life of someone you know, following the example and teaching of Christ.

4. What else do people use to push away the darkness of nightime? Make a list together, e.g. candles, electric light, fires . . . note how their effectiveness varies but they all perform the same function. What 'guiding light' does each of us use in daily life?

5. By day, of course, we have the great light, the Sun. It's there even when we cannot see it. Be grateful together for its light and heat, maintaining life. Remember that one great evidence of a blazing, bright sun is the shadow all around us! Can you and the children apply this to living?

6. Psalm 139 verses 11 and 12 – an amazing, wonderful thought to share at times of bewilderment and difficulty. Read it through to the children several times and just bask in God's great ability to give light.

7. There are, of course, degrees of light. Coming inside from the bright sunshine we have to pause and allow our eyes to adjust to what appears to be gloom – at first. But light is there, penetrating the building. So too there are degrees of understanding, seeing, living by truth. It is not a matter of either light or dark, so much as a growth in, a willingness to learn from, our own faith or light source. Older Juniors can discuss this learning process, facing specific moral and ethical issues.

Notes

Assembly 8: *Creation*

'Good morning to you all . . . we shall sing about the world, "And God said . . . " '(see p. 88 Appendix E).

'Yes, the Bible tells us that God spoke and one by one all things were made, they came into being. We call this the creation of the world, and we can read about it in the book of Genesis, which means beginnings.

> ZAP – Darkness was turned into light!
> ZAP – Flowers and trees arrived!
> ZAP – Animals and birds were about!

Some people think it all happened quickly like that . . . others think it took a long time. However it was, I believe God made it all . . . whether we do or don't, we can all agree it's a wonderful world . . . and where did it all come from? Why is it all here? . . . Just take time to consider that for yourselves . . .' (pause a while, no talking . . .)

And God continues to look after this beautiful world. What power was needed to make it - - - what power is needed to keep it going!

'Think of the **flowers** in your garden, all the various colours and shapes . . . in the school grounds like these . . . (bring in one or two samples that won't do any harm to pick.) . . . The trees towering above us as we play on the field, the blackberries you enjoy picking and eating in the woods . . . the bees that buzz about us and pollinate the plants . . . the little ants busy below ground . . . the tadpoles in the pond, the many birds singing in the fields and hedgerows . . .' (use any other examples from your own surroundings) 'and then of course there's your dog and cat at home . . . the cows who give us milk, the creatures in the sea, the sharks and shrimps, and the lions and tigers roaming in Africa and India . . . all made by God . . .'

(The list is endless, of course, and you make as much of this as you wish, collecting pictures and books, asking the children or classes to do so, in preparation or follow-up.)

'The great towering mountains, the rushing rivers, the crops in the field, the clouds overhead, the delicate snowflakes in winter, the stones beneath our feet, all so varied, and all created by a God of love. There's a little song I know:

> God who made the earth,
>   the air, the sky, the sea,
> who gave the light it's birth,
>   careth for me.

And that reminds me that he not only made and cares for everything, but looks after me too . . . and you . . . and you . . . and you (point briefly to all parts of the assembled children from one side to the other to make the point.)

'And he wants us, each of us, to look after this world together, caring for each other, and all the creatures, large and small. God made a world that was good and we must work to keep it a good place to be . . .'

'All the materials have been given to us to use sensibly – wood, clay for bricks, metals in the hills, minds to consider the answers to problems and questions . . . but *we* make nothing from nothing! Even when we create new plastics, we are only using what God has given us . . . only he actually made everything, gave the world existence, truly created it!

'I hope you can make this prayer your own now, . . . be still and ponder. . . . Lord, our great God, thank you for making such a good and glorious world . . . help us all to live in it wisely, to enjoy it, to share it, to care for it as you still do.'

'Let's sing another song. The wonders of creation are worth singing about' . . .

either 'God made the garden of creation' (song 16 in *Come and Praise*, London, BBC, 1978).

or 'Who put the colours in the rainbow?' (song 12 in *Come and Praise*, BBC).

Further ideas for assembly and class activities

1. Caring for the world – a vast subject! Whatever our religious beliefs we can all care for our environment. Ask the children to look around the school grounds for areas that can be looked after better. Ask them to prepare a list of suggestions that will provide animal habitats, protect plants, make the place more attractive and so on. Organise long and short term projects.

2. Looking carefully at a plant or small creature or the light playing on/changing a watery scene is to be encouraged. The details in a pattern or shape are truly wonderful and they are all around us, often missed by the children. They can draw what they observe too.

3. List together some of the wonders of creation that are within the children's immediate experience, e.g. the martins building their nests in the eaves of the houses, tadpoles turning into frogs, the colours of autumn leaves. Children can then present their own assembly on this theme, using research material, paintings etc.

4. 'Wonderful things we have seen on our holidays' is another good title for assembly. Perhaps ask each class to bring an item or two to share and everyone will enjoy a surprise!

5. Look at, read and compare creation stories from different religions/ethnic groups.

6. Design in nature is fascinating to explore. Look at how creatures are shaped, move, camouflaged, defend themselves and so on.

Notes

Assembly 9: *Measurement*

This assembly is part of a proposed school 'Measuring Week', preferably an introduction. Each class can undertake tasks on the theme, as the teachers see fit, and discoveries can be shared at a showing and sharing assembly (see Chapter 12).

Maths and Science co-ordinators will have an important role here too, pointing staff to suitable and challenging activities.

'We do a great deal of measuring in our world. (pause) How tall are you? What speed was she doing? How many sweets in the packet? How long will it take? are all examples of everyday questions.' (Move around as you speak, throwing the questions out to different parts of the hall.)

'Let's start today by listing all the different pieces of equipment we use to measure things.' (Have a **large sheet of white paper and a pen**, or **OHP transparency** ready.)

'Take those four questions first:
1. What could we use to measure a person's height? ' List items, e.g. ruler, tape measure.
2. 'What about the speed of a car? ' continue to add to the list, e.g. speedometer.
3. '. . . and the number of sweets? ' e.g. counting, just our brains and fingers or tally chart.
4. 'How long will it take?' e.g. watch, clock, even calendar!

Read back the list so far, compliment the children , and go on to ask, 'Now, what other things do we use to give us measurements?' List the items, commenting if necessary to encourage and open up new avenues e.g. 'What about temperature, no one's suggested how we measure that?'

You'll probably get a wide-ranging list.

'Well done everyone. Look now at the items, the equipment, on our list. We'll make a second list of the units of measurement. For example, here (point to word on list) we said a tapemeasure is used to measure height and length. When we have a measurement, what units do we use to say how much it was? . . . Yes, that's it, metres and centimetres.'

Start your list. 'What other units of measurement do we use? Look at our equipment list for help and ideas.'

In a lively, responsive manner talk as you list e.g. . . . 'thermometers, yes, give us temperatures in *degrees*, and we use *grams* and *kilograms* . . . good, you're right, sugar comes in 1kg packets, and. . . . what was that – decibels?!'

You may even have Newtons and candelas suggested! Let it be known that the lists can be added to as the 'measuring week' goes by.

'These are all agreed standard measurements (SI units for the initiated!) that help us understand size, weight and distance etc. etc. But what about things that are hard to measure . . . like worry?'

Start a third list on a **different coloured paper, or a mobile board**, to distinguish clearly from the others.

'We say things like 'I'm really worried', don't we? We try to measure, say how big or small these things are. What other things in life are difficult to quantify, or measure?'

Allow a pause for thought. Make your third list.

You may get suggestions like *safety, laziness, care, surprise, hope,*

Notes

kindness, curiosity, honesty, cruelty, beauty . . .
   The list could be quite amazing!
   Take a deep breath after all this list making . . . 'Phew, we have been busy. What a lot we've got to think about during our "measuring week"!'
   End your time together with a few quiet moments to think about what's been said and what will be discovered.

Further ideas for assembly and class activities

1. The feelings, attitudes, characteristics, conditions etc. listed are fascinating to discuss. We do try to quantify them by comparison and through experience, e.g. 'I was free as a bird,' or 'my fear knew no bounds' or 'he felt less sympathetic now'. . . . Do we need to measure them precisely anyway? If not, why not? Talk about this together.

2. Add to your lists during the week, everyday if you can. This keeps up a collective momentum. Refer to them briefly in each assembly.

3. Collect equipment that is used for measuring and display it in the hall, e.g. callipers, trundle wheels, stop watches. Perhaps ask a question about one item each day in assembly. Make sure they are handled and used.

4. Write out in *large* letters the list of units on separate pieces of paper and display them around the school. Older pupils can do this and put questions of their own beside them to stimulate interest.

5. Compile a list of things that you think are impossible to measure! This idea came from a pupil, and led to suggestions like galaxies, infinity, love, life and God. Sing:
   'Jesus' love is very wonderful
   So high you can't get over it
   So low you can't get under it
   So wide you can't get round it
   Oh, wonderful love.'
(No 31 in *Sing to God*, London, Scripture Union, 1971)

6. Don't forget to have a sharing assembly to tell each other what you have been measuring in your classes, and how you got on!

7. Make a collection of sayings using the word 'measure', e.g.
   He didn't measure up to expectations.
   For good measure, I added some more.
   It was made to measure.
   Or allied words, e.g. accuracy, estimate, quantity, capacity, amount, extent, size, dimension.

Assembly 10: *People are People*

As the children come into assembly play some **music** from one or two other countries (see Appendix A for details of UNICEF tape, if needed).

'This morning/afternoon we are thinking about people around the world. Did you listen to the music as you entered? Let's hear a little more . . . I wonder if you can recognise which country the music comes from?' Play a bit more of the CD/tape and see if they know the answer. If not, tell them, after a few suggestions.

'Making music, in many different ways, is one thing people all around the earth like to do. I wonder, what other things do all people, of all nations and tribes, have in common?' (repeat the question if necessary) 'Think about it . . . as you think, I would like 44 children* to come and do something!' (A set of multi-cultural tasks or international '**Happy Families**' cards is needed.)

'Put your hand up if you would like to help.' Choose class by class or row by row, or whatever is best for you. When they are all out the front (where space is, of course, essential) explain:

'I am going to give each one of you a card. There are four cards in each set and when I tell you to, you will move around, find the other three in your group and sit down as a set of four' (repeat slowly if required!). Give out the cards, look at everyone and be sure they understand. Then give the instruction 'Now get into your sets of four and sit down together in a space.' . . .

'Now these groups are all fours, but in real life, of course, it is not always like that, because groups vary.' Now ask a child, by name, to explain what group she/he is in. Try a second group as well. They will probably answer – 'The Chens', or 'The Singh group', or even more helpful 'The Da Silva *family*' . . . that's the word you want!

'Yes, you are all in family groups of four. Families from all parts of the world. Tell us your name and the country your cards have on them . . . ', ask one child in each group to answer so that all can hear. Perhaps repeat the list of countries yourself, slowly.

'Each of these groups has a Mr, a Mrs, a Miss and a Master (a girl and boy). Round the world different size family groups live and work together. So that's another thing all people share – family life, as well as work and music. What else can you think of . . .?'

Hopefully ideas like feelings, food, drink, clothes, fun, sport, homes will be suggested.

'What a lot people have in common, the similarities are many. So let's sing about what is happening now, "All over the world, everybody's building".' (No 61 in *Come and Praise 1 & 2*, London, BBC, 1978 & 1988 or No 59 in *Allelujah!*, London, A&C Black, 1980).

After the song say, 'Now let's all close our eyes and think of all the people round the world, who share the planet with us, and how we share in their lives and they in ours.'

---

* The number will vary, as you do not require more than 15–20% of the school! A large number though does make the activity very effective. The cards I used were a set published by Oxfam. If you make your own, adjust the number accordingly in multiples of four (see further ideas No 9). Boys and girls should be kept in equal numbers. If teachers are present they can help by sending a requested number from each of their classes, and 'guiding' the children if they have difficulty finding their group.

Further ideas for assembly and class activities

1. Having reminded each other of the similarities of the world's people, look at some of the differences together – skin colour, language, weather, styles of clothes, transport, income, types of food. Older children can discuss which are influenced by climate/geography, and which by other people.
2. Collect photos of people, especially crowds, from around the world. Display them so that similarities and differences can be searched out by the children and discussed.
3. Packs of A5 photographs from Oxfam are very useful:
   a) 'Where camels are better than cars' (a look at four different culture groups in Mali) £15.
   b) 'What is a family?' (raising questions of relationships, roles and structures) £12.50.
   c) 'Homes' (case studies from Malaysia, China and Scotland) £10.50
4. Children could write to Oxfam, UNICEF, Christian Aid, Tear Fund or Save the Children for help with their studies of certain countries or topics. Most materials are sold, but Christian Aid do produce some interesting free assembly suggestions, e.g. 'Specials Guests', 'Join the Celebration' and 'People friendly coffee.'
5. Read poems:
   'My new brother', Eric Finney and John Foster, *Orange Poetry Paintbox* (Oxford, OUP, 1996) p 61.
   'Cousins', John Rice, in his *Bears don't like Bananas* (London, Simon and Schuster, 1991) p 19.
   'My Gran visits England', Grace Nichols, in her *Give Yourself a Hug* (London, A&C Black, 1994) p 16.
   'One parent family', Moira Andrew, *Another Fifth Poetry Book* (Oxford, OUP, 1989) p 66.
6. Compiling a list of thoughts under the heading of 'Family to me is . . .', either individually or as a class, can be thought provoking.
7. What people have in common is growing more and more with modern communications. Think of a few together, e.g. styles of clothes and furnishings from all over the world, strange things like face-painting (once considered very primitive in Britain!).
8. Compose and play some music in a different style, e.g. Latin-American or tribal African. You may be able to borrow some unusual musical instruments from a Secondary School or a Music Resource Centre.
9. The Happy Families cards are useful for other prompters like the clothes, household items in the hands and food etc. The Oxfam set, which may help you make your own, was:

Family Name	Country	Family name	Country
Da Silva	Brazil	Singh	India
Chen	Hong-Kong	Ben Ali	Algeria
Motjeku	Lesotho	Shemma	Jordan
Trikas	Greece	Araneta	Philippines
Mokama	Botswana	Ikitok	Greenland
Patice	Dominica		

10. See also Assemblies 16 and 17.

Assembly 11: *Ironmongery Inspirations*

A title you may wish to ignore or to explain to the children, but chosen because it could lead you to think of other suitable items on which to base an assembly.

Ironmongery — 'tools and household articles, made of mainly metal.'

a) The Plumbline – 'I have something to show you today which you may not have seen.' Hold it up nice and high for everyone to see.

'Does anyone know what it is or how it's used?' . . . Your replies need to be acknowledged and then summarised. A child may know how it's used, but you will probably have to show this yourself.

'Well, this piece of string with a nicely balanced weight/mass at the end is called a plumbline. It has been used universally/all round the world for centuries, to help builders keep their constructions upright. It's truly international *and* ancient.

'As a wall was being built, the workers would use the plumbline to check it was standing-up straight/perpendicular. Like this . . . ' Take the plumbline over to a wall/doorpost/window and test them out (hopefully they will all be 'true'!).

'Anything that is not standing upright is shown to be crooked, or out of line, as we say.' (Any doorways etc. shown to be so you can point out, of course. Older buildings may help here in giving an example.)

Ask a child to use the plumbline and check a wall or partition, if you wish.

'There's a little story in the Bible which says,

'The Lord was standing by a wall that had been built true to plumb, with a plumbline in his hand. And the Lord asked me,

"What do you see, Amos?"

"A plumbline," I replied.

'Then the Lord said, "Look, I am setting a plumbline amongst my people Israel . . ." (Amos 7 verses 7&8)

Use the line again to show what this meant.

'God was telling his people, through Amos the messenger, that he was going to check-up on how honest and true they were. The message is for us today as well. God's plumbline is also international and always accurate.

'We may think that our lives are quite good when we compare them with other people. We all like to think we are not as bad as criminals, for example. But God measures us against Jesus, who was perfect in all he did and said, and then gave his life so that we could be forgiven.

'We are all found lacking when measured against Jesus, but the Christian faith and hope is based on the new start that Jesus brings for each of us. He enables us to live better lives.'

Sing Graham Kendrick's 'Servant King' (No 120, *Songs and Hymns of Fellowship*, Eastbourne, Kingsway, 1985) which begins 'From Heaven He came, helpless babe . . .'

'We end with a prayer – Thank you Lord, creator of all things, that Jesus came to this world to show us how to live, to bring us the power to follow his example and the forgiveness we always need.'

b) A Wind-vane (every school should have one, even if it's only plastic).

'Have a look at *this*.' (Show wind-vane clearly, proudly, even pompously!) 'What is it?' (Take the answers at a steady pace, some children will know its function, at least.)

'Right, yes, great! It shows us the direction of the wind. Like this, if wind is coming from the South towards the North (arrowhead pointing N) it will be pushed into this position.' (Move vane accordingly.)

'Where do you usually see this sort of equipment . . . they are called wind-vanes?' You'll probably get plenty of suggestions. 'That's it, on the tops of buildings, steeples of churches, even on poles in people's gardens. Who could come and move the arrow to show a wind coming from the East blowing towards the West?'

Wave your arms to show the directions. You may need, according to the age of the children, to spend a few moments explaining the four points of the compass and the corresponding letters on the vane (N, S, E & W). If intermediate points are marked you could use those as well with older Juniors, if you wish.

Presuming the arrow is moved correctly (pointing W) – 'Well done, thank you —————· Winds blow, you know, from all directions. For us, easterly winds often bring cold weather, and westerly winds usually bring rain. Now here's a short story.'

'Once two friends were out walking, enjoying a look around a pretty country village. They stopped at the local church and saw a wind-vane, like this one (point to yours), high up on the steeple. (Point up) On the point in the middle of the wind-vane they could *just* read the words put there – "God is love", it said. One of the friends said, "That's not correct, is it, God's love doesn't change like the wind; does it?" His companion thought for a moment, then replied, "You're right. The wind-vane shows us that God's love is certain, secure, always the same. Look up at the words, they are fixed, not moving, right in the middle of the wind-vane. Whatever direction the wind is coming from, God's love is there!" (Show the fixed centre point on your vane, where you may have a shape or figure instead.)

'The Bible tells us (Psalm 33:22) that "God's love is unfailing" and that we should trust in Him. We can all take comfort from this. Whatever direction the wind (spin the arrow), whatever 'the storms of life', the problems and pressures we face, God is LOVE.'

Further ideas for assemblies

1. Arising from a) read some of the chapters from Timothy Dudley-Smith's book *Stories of Jesus* (Lion) as an introduction to the life of Jesus.

2. Arising from b) look out for songs and poems, as a school, that tell of the love of God, and also perhaps, some stories about modern people who show his love in action. Enjoy sharing them with each other.

Notes

Assembly 12: *Practice Makes Perfect*

'I'm sure there's at least one thing at which we all want to improve . . . let me repeat that for you . . . I'm sure there's something at which we all want to improve . . . ' Watch the faces of the children, so you can ask of the nodding or smiling ones . . .

E.g. 'Think about it for yourself . . . yes, John, you are nodding, what do you want to improve? . . . Fine, your handwriting, well done.' Take a few more personal suggestions, repeating them.

'What does it *mean* to improve?' (listen to a few answers) 'Yes, to get better at it, which is very satisfying. How do we do that? How can John improve his handwriting, or Judith get better at making her bed?' etc. etc.

Take a few ideas. You will probably get answers like: trying harder, doing it more, practising, getting help, asking to be shown. Use these as you continue. (Other ideas like 'getting a better pen' can be acknowledged as possibilities, but not highlighted!) 'Yes, I think you're right. It takes effort and practice to get better at something. We may need advice or help as well to show us exactly what we need to improve. Take the example of the knight in *Alice Through the Looking Glass* (Lewis Carroll, Chapter 8 'It's my own invention', London, Penguin, 1994). Read (with smiles!) your own abbreviated version (beginning at 'whenever the horse stopped . . .').

'He did try to gear his practice to meet his own needs, using a horse on wheels, but was it helping him, do you think?' Take some responses and then sum them up in your own words, e.g. 'The knight was trying hard, it may have been of use, but perhaps practice on the real thing would have been better. For him though, it seems to have helped a bit by giving him confidence.' Share a smile here!

'So with us, whatever we want to get better at, we must stop and think – 'How can I do this?' 'What exactly should I be practising so I do improve?' Maybe talk to someone about it as well, to make sure you are not wasting your energy and time. We all need to think about exactly what to practice. Be precise and then work at that skill.

'There's a saying, *Practice makes Perfect*. What do you think of that? Can practice *make* perfect? Could you improve your handwriting and ─────── (add whatever other examples have been given) that much?'

Listen to a few replies, which may vary a good deal, but will give you a positive note to end on!

'Whatever you want to improve, practise often, and I'm sure your efforts will be rewarded . . . there's always room for improvement.'

Sing – 'Wake up each day', *Allelujah!* No 60 (London, A&C Black, 1960).
or 'One More Step' – perhaps two selected verses, *Come and Praise* No 47 (London, BBC, 1978).

Notes

Further ideas for assembly and class activities

1. How will efforts for improvement be seen as successful? Children can discuss this, identifying their own criteria. Often there is a little success at first and many stages on the way. Consider together the first faltering steps of a toddler, the taking of that first unaided step, the many tumbles on the way – but we learn to walk! Or think about the learning of a musical skill over a period of time. At first odd, even unattractive noises, but with patience and regular practice tunes are learnt and more complicated, lovely pieces are performed. Encourage your guitar or recorder players to share experiences of improving their performance. Perhaps a peripatetic music teacher can help in this too.

2. 'Big oaks from little acorns grow' – another saying to think about together.

3. Look at OHP transparency 15. The osprey catching his fish. Talk about how this skill is learned – observation, trial and error, practice of timing, flying, diving etc. A real life wonder in itself.

4. Ask the children to consider what they now do as 'second nature', out of habit, that once they struggled with and had to practise e.g. riding a bike or peeling potatoes. Celebrate these achievements together.

5. Alice's world was a strange one. In the real world, practice does help over time. A lot can be achieved. Ask for some *outstanding* stories of improvement and success about each other from the children and the staff. This is a real source of encouragement and affirmation that shows an appreciation of one another.

6. Can the school identify something that as a community it needs to improve by practice, agree the stages and then monitor the success? e.g. coming into assembly sensibly, caring for the birds in winter.

7. Read the lovely story in the poem 'The Magical Bicycle', Berlie Doherty in her anthology *Walking on Air* (London, Harper Collins Lions, 1993) p 16.

Notes

Assembly 13: *Fantasy and Imagination*

'*Fantasy* is . . . ' Ask a child to read a definition from a **dictionary**, e.g. 'the faculty or ability to invent images, especially extravagant or visionary ones; a fanciful mental image, a daydream'.

'Sounds exciting doesn't it? And how about this, ***imagination*** is . . . ' Ask a second pupil to read, e.g. 'a mental faculty forming images or concepts of external objects not present to the senses, the ability of the mind to be creative or resourceful.' (Both from *Oxford Encyclopaedic Dictionary*, Oxford, OUP, 1991.)

'Wow! What a wonderful gift this is! And we all have this power in our minds to create unusual pictures, relive experiences. We each control the pictures we see in our minds.

'Try now, to imagine in your mind a seaside scene or another place where you would like to go again.'

A few moments of stillness and quiet.

'Would anyone describe to us what they are seeing, touching, in their mind's eye, in their imagination?' Take a few replies, trying to involve girls and boys, all age groups. Repeat each description briefly so everyone hears. Keep a steady exciting, yet calm pace.

'Wonderful isn't it, the powers we have to fantasise like this? We can actually be in two places at once! Be careful though. One of the explanations was daydreaming. What does that mean do you think?'

Again listen to 4/5 ideas and summarise in your own words, e.g. 'Yes, it's usually when we let our mind wander off and think of other things, when we have a job we should be doing.'

'But, although we must use it wisely, do we imagine creatively as often as we might? Look at this **picture**' – either show a Salvador Dali print, or an unusual pattern/painting by a pupil.

'Here, out-of-the-ordinary connections are being made, to create something different and startling, even extravagant. Daydreaming, picture-making . . . how else can we use our imaginations?' Ask for a few suggestions; most likely are writing stories and poems, making models, playing with toys, dolls, puppets and perhaps inventing things/machines.

'C.S. Lewis, the famous story writer, once said that using our imagination "is bringing to the boil, what God left on simmer". It's rather like turning up the heat, putting effort into our minds. Let's be still and quiet for a few moments, and be thankful for our powers of fantasy and imagination that can take us into other worlds.'

After the time of thoughtfulness, encourage the children to really bring their imaginations to the boil during their lives to create pictures, stories, poems, models etc.; then sing a favourite song to finish.

Notes

Special Times ASSEMBLY 13

Further ideas for assembly and class activities

1. Imagination often thrives in quiet, lonely spells. We all need time to 'daydream'. Times of isolation can be treasured rather than feared. Tell the children about John Bunyan in prison on the bridge at Bedford writing *Pilgrim's Progress* and Astrid Lingren, who was inspired to create *Pippi Longstocking* whilst confined to her bed for long periods. Powers of imagination helped them through difficult times. Read extracts from their books.

2. The children's own stories and poems can be read in assembly, of course. You may like to have a 'special season of fantasy' when the children can share how and when their ideas came to them.

3. Scientific discovery also needs an element of vision. Albert Einstein (1879–1955) said quite openly that 'the gift of fantasy' was important in his work. Isaac Newton (1642–1727) when asked how he discovered the wonders of the colour spectrum and gravity, remarked that he was 'always thinking about it'. Children could find out more about these two great men; for neither of them was progress easy, they had to strive for success.

4. The Narnia stories of C. S. Lewis are the product of a very fertile imagination. Read extracts and discuss the plots of one or two. The *Silver Chair* is particularly appealing.

5. There are plenty of weird and wonderful poems to enjoy these days. Dip into James Reeves' and Edward Ardizzone's *Prefabulous Animiles* (London, Heinemann, 1957), *Fizzy, Whizzy Poetry Book* by John Cunliffe (London, Scholastic, Young Hippos, 1995), and Michael Rosen's *Pilly Soems* (London, A&C Black, 1994).

6. Ask the children to look at some of Salvador Dali's paintings and then create one of their own in his style. Talk about the terms 'abstract' and 'subconscious' with older pupils who are interested.

Notes

Assembly 14: *Obsessions*

Perhaps a very unusual subject for a Primary assembly. It is a difficult subject to deal with, but in these days of mass media, peer pressure and image promotion, one worth attempting. Middle and upper Juniors (about ages 8–12) are particularly vulnerable, and airing the subject may help some youngsters in their teenage years.

'Hobbies and interests are great to have. They broaden our view of life. But sometimes things can take over our lives, almost haunt us, so that they dominate us and stop us thinking of and doing other things. This we can call an obsession.'

'Obsessions push everything else out and can even prevent us eating and sleeping properly. The one thing is continually in our mind to the exclusion of all else, and life becomes unbalanced for us. . . . They can take many forms – people, styles of dress, a worry or even at first, a passing fad.'

'Let me read you a story to show what I mean. As you listen, think about the main character and what life has become for him.'

Read either **The Story of a Motor Fan** by H.A. Field (in *Carry on Reading* Blue Book 5, p 83, Huddersfield, Schofield and Sims, 1977).

or **Albert Blows a Fuse** (a cautionary tale for television addicts) by Tom Bower (Oxford, Lion, 1991) *Stop* at the arrival of the pink bird in the grey room.

The first, although maybe more difficult to obtain, is to be preferred because it is a bit further removed from the lives of the children.

'That, you see, is what obsession, does – so sad and futile. If one thing takes over like that, think of everything else that is being missed . . . Well then, what did you think about this story?'

Allow the children time for a pause, to gather their feelings and ideas, then see if one or two will respond. Summarise their observations, once about 6–10 have spoken. If all is quiet, do not 'push' for children to speak, just say, 'Well, there's something to think about, if not now then in the future, as you grow up.'

If you read the Albert story, you could go on to finish it if there's time, because the situation does change.

NOTE: Both examples are clearly fictitious, and it would be unfair and injudicious to be precise about particular obsessions.

On a lighter note, end with singing 'Lord I love to stamp and shout' (No 5 *Someone's Singing, Lord*, London, A&C Black, 1973).

Notes

Further ideas for assembly and class activities

1. Pick up the positive strains of the song. Look together at all the wonderful activities one can enjoy and rejoice in the variety! Discuss what appeals to each of you and why.

2. Have a hobbies day. Each child brings in something to show and talk about briefly, e.g. a riding hard-hat, a stamp collection, a gerbil, some models, a musical instrument. The possibilities are endless and it is always amazing what interests there are. This, of course, spreads ideas and helps everyone.

3. 'Variety is the spice of life' – a saying to discuss together – is it true? Give each other reasons, for and against the proposition, with reference to the story.

4. What we think about affects what we are and do, in the same way that what we eat affects our health. Think about this together in an RE lesson and refer to St Paul's suggestions in Philippians 4 verse 8.

5. Make a school collection of leaflets, catalogues, posters, newspaper cuttings – over a longish period – to show the range of hobbies, clubs and societies locally available to the youngsters and their families.

6. First, as teachers, review your policy for a provision of extra-curricular clubs. Then ask the children what else would interest them, what perhaps could stop for a while. Take action accordingly, bearing in mind the pressures you already have to endure! Older Juniors can run clubs for younger pupils in small groups – with a little teacher supervision – and maybe parents can help too.

7. Read a poem or two, e.g. 'Bounce-a-ball at Playtime', Wes Magee, *Purple Poetry Paintbox* (Oxford, OUP, 1996) p 41.
'Seaside in Winter' by Daphne Lister, *Orange Poetry Paintbox* (Oxford, OUP, 1996) p 13.
'How to Treat the House-plants', Kit Wright in his *Hot Dog and Other Poems* (London, Puffin, 1992) p 42.
'The Useful Art of Knitting' by Katherine Craig, *Another Second Poetry Book*, ed. John Foster (Oxford, OUP, 1988) p 52.
'Conker Crazy', Pie Corbett, *Sandwich Poets* – Rice, Corbett and Moses (London, Macmillan, 1995) p 52.

8. The children can write their own 'cautionary tales' about obsessions, e.g. 'He was football crazy' or 'She was in a world of her own', with a very vivid warning for each other!

Assembly 15: *The Rainbow*

This can link with Assembly 1, 'The Wonder of Colour', as part of a series, or stand on its own with a different emphasis.

Listen first to the song 'Oh, what a wonderful scene, the rainbow overhead . . . ' (King's Singers version is very good, but there are others. It's from *Captain Noah and His Floating Zoo*, a short musical by Michael Flanders and Joseph Horovitz – the last song).

It's quite short, so if everyone is attentive, hear it through a second time, then ask – 'So, what do you think our assembly is about today?' Don't forget to smile!

As ever, a good set of varied answers will be given. Based on the song, suggestions like 'colours, seeing the rainbow' should be forthcoming, so continue:

'Lovely, a lot of ideas there. The song, in fact, comes right at the end of the musical version of the story of Noah.' Hold up the record or cassette sleeve if you have it. 'It's called *Captain Noah and His Floating Zoo*, and we are going to hear the story read to us.'

Use *Lion Story Bible, Book 3* – 'Noah' (Oxford, 1992), which is suitable for a few older children and some teachers to read a portion each. To keep the flow, this should be practised beforehand.

If you prefer, the Good News Bible version can be read, e.g. Genesis chapter 9 verses 12–16. This is only the promise at the end of the adventure, so you need to select earlier verses or tell the story in your own way.

'As the song said, *the rainbow was a sign of promise*. After the terrible flood, the rainbow appeared for the very first time, just as we sometimes see one after a storm or heavy rain, and the sun shines through. The seasons each year are promised as certain and reliable, for all the earth to enjoy.'

'The story comes in the first book of the Bible, called Genesis, which means beginnings (pause). What are the seasons of the year? Who can tell us one of them?' Take one suggestion from each child answering, affirming as you go. Continue until you hopefully have all four, but don't take too long.

'Well done, our seasons are summer, autumn, winter and spring . . . and God promises they will continue, so life can go on, so seedtime and harvest can continue. The Rainbow is very beautiful and reminds us all of God's unfailing love. Put your hand up if you have ever seen a rainbow . . . wonderful! . . . put two hands up if you have seen a rainbow on more than one occasion . . . look at that! . . . so many of us have seen the sign of promise!

'Now let's be very quiet and in our own hearts and minds say thank you, for the rainbow, a beautiful sign of promise'. Allow a few moments before asking the children to leave.

A picture or painting of a rainbow is useful to have and show at the end of assembly, as you play the music again for the children to leave.

Notes

Further ideas for assembly and class activities

1. Read Joan Aiken's story *The Last Slice of the Rainbow* in the book of the same name (London, Jonathan Cape, 1985).
2. The children can paint a large rainbow. The colours of the spectrum are not the same as the song, so be sure to get the order correct first!

3. Ask the children – 'How is a rainbow formed?' The story of the Flood gives clues of course, and perhaps some will be able to explain how the sun shines through the water droplets in the clouds and the light is refracted.

4. Make some prisms and Newton's discs available for the children to see, handle and experiment with.

5. Investigate colours that are used as signs or symbols, e.g. Red – stop and Green – go (from traffic lights); Blue for cold; Gold for success or wealth.

6. Children can write a poem about their favourite colour, or one using the format 'Yellow is . . .' and proceeding to list things like bananas, being afraid, mum's creamy custard etc. They can choose their own colours, of course.

7. Make, or get older children to make, six cards (approx. 60 x 10 cm) with the words – WINTER, SUMMER, AUTUMN, SPRING, SEEDTIME, HARVEST – written on them in large clear letters. Use them in an assembly, held by six children, and ask the school to put them in order, giving instructions clearly when asked to help by you. Organise and develop this in your own way!

8. Older pupils can investigate why Archbishop Desmond Tutu uses the title 'The Rainbow People' for the freed people of the new South Africa.

Notes

Assembly 16: BIG and small

Act the parts of two children, straight in, no introductions.

'I'm bigger than you, so *I'll* do it!' Looking down, and pushing the other child aside.

'Hey, why should you? That's not fair!' Looking up plaintively.

'Ever heard a conversation like that? I'm absolutely sure you have. But what does it mean – bigger than you? Is it just physical size, or age, or experience and skill that counts?'

'And what is the job to be done? A smaller person can crawl through a hole in a fence more easily, where a taller, larger person would get stuck!'

'We all have different abilities and our bodies are quite different in size too, they develop at different rates. Let's sing a song about ourselves – "I can climb the highest mountain . . . I'm happy to be me" (No 17 in *Every Colour Under the Sun*, London, Ward Lock, 1983).

'Yes, we should each be happy to be ourselves. But what about this business of being *big*? I'm going to ask each teacher to send two children from their class out to the front, who would like just to say one thing that they are good at . . . '

Ask each teacher in turn to send two children to the front who have volunteered (ask them to arrange this the day before if you wish).

Presuming you have 10–20 children, a manageable group, ask each to say just briefly in one sentence something they think they are good at. Ensure the line is of all ages and heights in a random order at this stage.

'Thank you, very interesting. Now we must all try to remember who is good at what! All right, we'll ask them again to tell us, in one word this time!' Call each child's name in rapid succession, so that the words fly back quickly, e.g. 'football . . . writing . . . drawing . . . dancing . . . maths . . .

'Now please arrange yourselves in order, tallest at this end (point) and shortest at that (point).' Allow a few moments, and enlist the aid of a teacher or helper, if needed, to speed things up.

'Well done. We can clearly see that of these children, X is the tallest, but Y next to him is still good at ——— and Z here is good at – what? (take replies) yes, ———, although he is smaller than A and B.'

You will have to insert the names and skills yourself, and by looking at the row make whatever points you can about the unimportance of physical size.

'Thank you, sit down where you are. Does size matter, do you think? . . . I'm bigger than all of these children, and an elephant is bigger than me! A mouse is tiny compared with an elephant, but massive to an ant, who is still a very clever creature nonetheless! It all depends on how we view things. Listen finally to this poem . . . '

Read 'Giants' by Lydia Pender, in her anthology *Morning Magpie*, p 64 (Sydney, Angus & Robertson, 1984) or 'Large and Small ' by Daphne Lister, in *Red Poetry Paintbox*, p 26, ed. John Foster (Oxford, OUP, 1994).

'Think on! and keep your view of yourself in proportion. We can't take credit for our size, but we can for the way we work and behave.'

Notes

Further ideas for assembly and class activities

1. How big do we look from outer space?!
   Using photos of:
   - the planet earth
   - a group of planets
   - the Milky Way

   think of the size of one person in comparison!
   Yet God cares for us all and each one individually (use Psalm 8 vv 3&4 and Luke 12 vv 6&7).

2. Another song to sing and consider is 'Hundreds and thousands – yet God knows me' (No 18 in *Sing to God*, London, Scripture Union, 1971).

3. Some poems to read and enjoy:
   'Sometimes, I Pretend', Trevor Harvey, *Yellow Poetry Paintbox* (Oxford, OUP, 1994) p 34.
   'Elephant and Ant', John Foster, *Red Poetry Paintbox*, ed. John Foster (Oxford, OUP, 1994) p 28.
   'Giant', Irene Yates, *Red Poetry Paintbox*, ed. John Foster (Oxford, OUP, 1994) p 31.

4. Collect things from around the school that can be arranged in size, e.g. books, balls. Does size alter the function appreciably?

5. Together look up some of the 'biggest' and 'smallest' listed in the *Guinness Book of Records*.

6. As far as people are concerned and the way they relate to one another, consider what we mean by being 'big' or 'grown-up'. Physical, emotional, mental and spiritual values can be investigated.

7. In groups, compose some music with appropriate instruments, to describe the movement of tiny creatures and large creatures (chosen by the children after some discussion).

8. See also Assemblies 10 and 17.

Notes

Assembly 17: *Personalities are Different*

This links naturally with Assemblies 10 and 16.
Ref: Acts 10 verse 34 – 'God shows no favouritism.'

As the children enter the hall, place on the **table** before them a **large glass tumbler filled with coloured water**, then a **second glass** (of the same size) beside it **half-filled with water of the same colour**.

Once everyone is settled, begin, 'Yes, we have two objects before us today, have a look at them and be ready to say exactly what you see.' Now stand behind the table and lift up the full glass. Ask, 'What am I holding here?' Take a good range of answers. If necessary, make comments as you go to keep the suggestions coming, e.g. 'Lovely, yes, James says it's blue glass, and Jenny has added she thinks it's some sort of coloured liquid in a tumbler.'

The more ideas you can speedily collect, the better. With a 'Thank you, well done everyone,' proceed to hold up the half-filled glass and ask ponderously, 'So, what do we think we have here, what am I holding now?'

Go round and gather a variety of responses again. The general opinion will probably be a glass half-filled with blue water/liquid, but someone may say 'it is half-empty'. Affirm all contributions, and if needed tip half the liquid from the first glass into the second, and holding up the first glass ask again, 'What am I holding up now?' You may get some new descriptions!

Whatever the observations from the children, then go on, 'We are all looking at the same two objects. As we think of words to describe what we see, we often explain things differently. Which is good, we help each other that way. It is quite correct to say this glass (hold it up again) is half empty, and it is quite correct to say it is half-full.'

Put onto the **OHP**, or write on a **board** –

People are different
People see things in different ways

Read the words as you write them. 'We all need to realise this. Sometimes it can be that . . .' Read the words again and add 'very' to both sentences as you do. So now it looks like this –

very
People are ∧ different

very
People see things in ∧ different ways

'Sometimes people are so noticeably different that they even "stick-out" as we say, like the words "very" here. We must accept this, be ourselves, and listen carefully to different ideas. Being tolerant we can call this – that is allowing others to have different opinions and ideas without teasing or laughing at them. We won't all laugh at the same jokes, or enjoy the same food. We have different hobbies, different ways of doing things. Different people can be upset by different things. So let's be aware of this, and try to be patient and tolerant with each other.'

'We will be still and quiet for a few moments . . . (continue once all are settled) and be thankful and happy that we have a variety of people in the world, and here at school. We are different on the outside and on the inside. Let's rejoice in our different personalities and ask God to help us appreciate each other.' . . .

Maybe sing to finish – 'I can climb the highest mountain' (song 17 in *Every Colour Under the Sun*, London, Ward Lock, 1983), asking the children to realise afresh that each of us should be happy we *can* be ourselves and let others be themselves as individuals too.

Further ideas for assembly and class activities

1. The story of the Good Samaritan can be read (Luke 10 vv 25–38), emphasising that:
   1) the parable was told in answer to the question 'who is my neighbour?', and
   2) that the Samaritans were not treated properly or tolerated fairly by the Jews. Then discuss together.

2. Some poems to read:
   'Things I'm not good at' by Jeff Moss, *Me and You and Poems 2*, ed. Rolf Harris (London, Knight Books, 1993) p 32.
   'My obnoxious brother' by Colin West, *Me and You and Poems 2*, ed. Rolf Harris (London, Knight Books, 1993) p 172.
   'Playground Problems' by Eric Finney, *Orange Poetry Paintbox* ed. John Foster (Oxford, OUP, 1996) p 18.
   'Kicking Turf' by Pie Corbett, *Sandwich Poets* by Rice, Corbett and Moses (Basingstoke, Macmillan, 1995) p 58.
   'I'm Different' by John Cunliffe, *Fizzy Whizzy Poetry Book* (London, Scholastic, Young Hippos, 1995) p 44.

3. Ask the children to write about a friend, mentioning not only what they have in common, but where there are differences of opinion, interests or taste etc.

4. There's an interesting little book called *It's okay to be different* by Sally Jordan and Diana Philbrook (Cincinnati, Ohio, Standard Publishing, 1986) that's worth trying to track down for ideas.

5. Show the children some 'double-perception pictures' to further illustrate what can be seen in different ways, e.g. the famous Rubin's Vase, Muller-Lyer illusion and Leeper's 'Ambiguous Lady' (you should be able find these in a standard psychology text book). Some holograms and 'magic eye' pictures can also be used for fun to discover who can see what.

6. Listen to and/or sing 'You'll always have a friend in me', from the Disney *Toy Story* film, available in video. Two toys bury their differences to pull together in a crisis!

7. Do some research to show some differences between all the children in the school, e.g. a favourite colour or an answer to a question like, 'do you agree with zoos?' Present, analyse and discuss the results as you think appropriate. Perhaps consider whether these differences stop you working together.

8. Older Juniors can discuss the meaning and application of words like *prejudice, caricature, stereotype & discrimination*, as well as *personality*.

9. Some of these issues could be discussed in class or group 'Circle Time'.

Assembly 18: *Promises, Promises*

'A promise *is* a promise, we sometimes say. So what do you think a promise is? What does it mean to make a promise?'

Plenty of hands will probably shoot up to answer. Asking a range of ages, boys and girls, and perhaps a teacher, parent or other adult, try to get a good lot of precise, instant responses. Thank each contributor and summarise in your own way what you have heard.

E.g. 'Excellent – we think a promise is saying we will definitely do something, someone can rely on it. Like a guarantee, it is an assurance that something will or will not happen . . . ' A pause and a smile '. . . so, who has made a promise today? Hands up!' If there are a dozen or so responses take the answers, if not add . . . 'Well, if not today, who has made a promise in the last few days? . . . quite a lot, keep your hand up if you would like to tell us to whom you made the promise and what it was . . . '

Most probably it will be to Mum, Dad or another member of the family, some may even say they promised themselves or God. As you listen to the answers, pick out 5 or 6 different ones to come back to (write names down, or ask a teacher to do so if you need help).

'Thank you all very much. Lots of promises to choose from, some have been kept already I suspect. Now, would ____,____,____ (name 5/6 you selected) please stand up. I am going to ask you to repeat your promise and to whom you made it, and then would you please say if you sincerely think you will keep it.'

Your choice of children clearly depends on your knowledge of them and the promises given, as you see best. Ask them slowly, one by one . . .

E.g. 'John, your promise was . . . (wait for an answer) and you gave it to . . . (wait again) and do you think you will be able to keep it?! ' . . . perhaps with a smile, or questioning look! Respond accordingly yourself, such as 'Very good, I'm glad you are so sure', or 'Yes, it may be rather hard!'

Most children who help you will be keen to keep the promises, which will probably be realistic in the main.

'All worth thinking about . . . We should all try to make only the promises we can keep, to match our actions to our words. Listen carefully to this story, now . . . '

Read 'The Two Sons' (from *Stories Jesus Told* series by Nick Butterworth and Mick Inkpen, Heathcote, Picture Lions, Collins, 1994). This is a lovely re-telling of the little story in Matthew 21 verses 28–32. If you can't get hold of the book, tell the Bible story in your own words.

'Neither actually was true to his word, but for one that was good, for another it was sad!'

Either end with a moment of **quiet** to think about making or keeping promises, or **sing** 'Can you be sure that the rain will fall?' (No 31, *Come and Praise 1 & 2*, London, BBC, 1978 & 1988).

Notes

Further ideas for assembly and class activities

1. The children's responses to the 'Two Sons' story can be shared and discussed – what a surprise ending!

2. Ask the children what advice they would give to a younger sister or brother about making promises to people.

3. The song suggested begins –
    'Can you be sure that the rain will fall?
    Can you be sure that the birds will fly?
    Can you be sure that the rivers will flow?
    Or that the sun will light the sky?
    God has promised, God never breaks
    a promise He makes, His word is always true.'
   All these natural events are sure because God is reliable and keeps the world in order. Ask the children what specific promises they know God has made (see Assembly 15).

4. A few poems to use:
   'What Me?' by Brian Morse in his anthology *Plenty of Time* (London, Bodley Head, 1994) p 51.
   'The Gerbil' by Tony Bradman in Rolph Harris' *Me and You Poems 2* (London, Knight Books, 1993) p 150.
   'An Urgent Call to the Dentist' by John Cunliffe in his *Fizzy Whizzy Poetry Book* (London, Scholastic, Young Hippos, 1995) p 34.

5. 'Promises, Promises' – ask the children to write a poem or story with this title, about promises given and broken or kept, and how this made people feel.

Notes

18 POSTSCRIPT

Not everything that happens in assembly will meet with everyone's full agreement (not even the Head's) all the time. But that's reality, and so be it. There will be difficulties to sort out. We did have noise from the kitchen, fidgeting children and interruptions to live with, and try to eradicate. We experimented with afternoon assemblies and different sitting arrangements and had our failures too. But through it all, the creativity of the staff and children was inspiring. These were special times.

The law of the land tells us our times of worship in school should 'accord a special place to Jesus', so as an appropriate ending to this book of shared ideas we quote his own words, 'By their fruits, you shall know them' (Matt 7:20); 'I am the vine; you are the branches . . . apart from me you can do nothing' (John 15:5).

Appendix A

A Brief Recommended Booklist

GENERAL

UNICEF, Book of children's Games and Songs from Around the World (with cassette). Catalogue from 55, Lincoln's Inn Fields, London, WC2A 3NB.
Children Just Like Me (London, Dorling Kindersley, 1995).
Scope for Reading – Books 1, 2 & 3 (Huddersfield, Schofield and Sims, 1978); some good passages for reading aloud.
Lion Book of Children's Prayers, Mary Bachelor (Oxford, Lion, 1984).
365 Children's Prayers, Carol Watson (Oxford, Lion, 1989).
Multi-cultural:
  Let's Celebrate – Festivals (Oxford, OUP, 1989)
  Celebrations, Chris Deshpande (London, A&C Black, 1994).
  Storyworlds Books 1&2, Richard Brown (London, Oliver & Boyd, 1988).
Leading Little Ones to God, Marion Schoolland (London, Banner of Truth, 1970).
Lion Handbook to the Bible (Oxford, Lion Publishing, 1973).
Lion Book of Stories of Jesus, Timothy Dudley-Smith (Oxford, Lion Publishing, 1986).
Oxford Book of Christmas Stories ed. Dennis Pepper (Oxford, OUP 1988).
You Can Change the World, Jill Johnstone (Carlisle, OM Books, 1993).
A Young Person's Guide to Saving the Planet, Debbie Silver & Bernadette Vallely (London, Virago Press, 1990). A very informative ABC about caring for the environment.
You and Me series by Althea (London, A&C Black, 1996).
That's not Fair, Barry & Trish Miller (RMEP) – resources for exploring moral education (Exeter, Pergamon, 1990).
Creation Stories retold by Maureen Stewart (London, Hodder & Stoughton).
The Story of Creation, The Story of Christmas, Jane Ray (London, Orchard Books, 1991 & 1992).

POETRY COLLECTIONS (specifically for assembly use)

Wheel Around the World, compiled by Chris Searle (London, Macdonald, 1983).
Bears Don't Like Bananas, John Rice (London, Simon and Schuster, 1991).
Conkers, poems by Barrie Wade (Oxford, OUP, 1989).
Oxford Book of Christmas Poems, eds. Michael Harrison and Christopher Stuart-Clark (Oxford, OUP, 1983).
Oxford Treasury of Children's Poetry, ed. Michael Harrison (Oxford, OUP, 1988).
Another Second Poetry Book, ed. John Foster (Oxford, OUP, 1988).
Another Third Poetry Book, ed. John Foster (Oxford, OUP, 1988).
Another Fourth Poetry Book, ed. John Foster (Oxford, OUP, 1988).

Special Times

Another Fifth Poetry Book, ed. John Foster (Oxford, OUP, 1989).
Morning Magpie, Lydia Pender (Sydney, Angus and Robertson, 1984). A refreshing anthology from Australia.
Wordscapes, Barry Maybury (Oxford, OUP, 1970). (Out of print.)
Thoughtscapes, Barry Maybury (Oxford, OUP, 1972). (Out of print.)
Poetry Plus – Book one A Diary of Poems, B. R. Marney, M. Hussamy, A. N. Ashton, S. M. Parle (Huddersfield, Schofield and Sims, 1982). A useful through the year selection.
A Word in Season, Prose and poetry for use in Christian education and worship, compiled by D. Hilton (Redhill, NCEC, 1984). (Out of print.)
A Footprint on the Air, nature verse, selected by Naomi Lewis (London, Knight Books, 1983).
Heard it in the Playground, Alan Ahlberg (London, Puffin, 1991). Real life in a primary school!
Stuff and Nonsense, Gordon Bailey (Oxford, Lion Publishing, 1989). Thought-provoking humour for upper Juniors.
Hot Dog and Other Poems, Kit Wright (London, Puffin, 1982).
Sandwich Poets – Rice, Corbett and Moses, John Rice, Pie Corbett and Brian Moses (Basingstoke, Macmillan, 1995).
Give Yourself a Hug, Grace Nichols (London, A&C Black, 1994). Lively characters and seasonal tastes.
Noisy Poems, collected by Jill Bennett (Oxford, OUP, 1987).
Quick! Let's Get Out of Here, Michael Rosen and Quentin Blake (London, Puffin, 1985).
You Tell Me, Roger McGough and Michael Rosen (London, Puffin, 1985).
A Mouse in My Roof, Richard Edwards (London, Puffin, 1990).
Me and You Poems – 2, Rolf Harris (London, Knight Books, 1993).
Green Poetry, Ed. Robert Hull (Hove, Wayland, 1993).
Dove on the Roof – a collection of poems about Peace selected by Jennifer Currey (London, Mammoth, 1992).
Let's Celebrate – Festival poems, ed. John Foster (Oxford, OUP, 1989).
Word Play, with a section on friends (London, BBC, 1992). (Out of print.)
Christmas Poetry, Robert Hull (Hove, Wayland, 1993).
Walking on Air, Berlie Doherty (London, Collins, Young Lions, 1993).
Wondercrump Poetry, ed. J. Curry (London, Red Fox, 1994).
Rhymes for Annie Rose, Shirley Hughes (London, Bodley Head, 1995).
Plenty of Time, Brian Morse (London, Bodley Head, 1994).
Poetry Paintbox series (Red, Yellow, Green, Blue – Oxford, OUP, 1994; Purple, Orange – Oxford, OUP, 1996).
Out of the Blue (weather poems), ed. Fiona Waters (Oxford, Collins, 1982).
Ten Bananas More, ed. Sally Bacon and Susan Blisten, Poetry Society (London, Simon and Schuster, 1994)

Appendix B

Songbooks

Sing to God – Scripture Union (London, 1971).
Merrily to Bethlehem – A&C Black (London, 1978).
Carol, Gaily Carol – A&C Black (London, 1973).
Allelujah! – A&C Black (London, 1980).
Someone's Singing Lord – A&C Black (London, 1973).
Apusskidu – A&C Black (London, 1975).
Come and Praise – BBC (London, 1970) & Book 2 (London, 1988).
Every Colour Under the Sun – Ward Lock (London, 1983).

Other Resources

Slides
a. **of Holy Land**, available from: Bible Lands Society, PO Box 50, High Wycombe, Bucks, HP15 7QU.
b. **of other countries round the world** from: Commonwealth Institute, Kensington High Street, London, W8 6NQ (0171 603 4545).

Posters
With attractive pictures and wise/witty texts can be bought from Argus: Antioch Ltd., Pipers Lane Estate, Thatchman, Berks RG19 4NA.
Or Palm Tree posters from Kevin Mayhew Ltd., Rattlesden, Bury St. Edmunds, Suffolk IP30 O52.
Tear Fund (101 Church Road, Teddington Middlesex, TW11 8QE), do a useful set of international photos linked with the 'I am' sayings of Jesus, and other audio/video resources.

Intermediate Technology, Myson House, Railway Terrace, Rugby, CV21 3HT.
The Zimbabwe Hoe (see p 38) and many other real-life technology solutions from the 'third world' are available in a regular newsletter to supporters. Well worth considering – Technology Co-ordinator take note!

Appendix C

Some Children's Answers
(From the children of Broomgrove Junior School, Wivenhoe, Essex 1986 – 1992).

1. What is worship? -

- realising worth
- honouring
- praising
- praying to God
- being friendly
- serving
- singing
- obeying
- merit
- adoring
- thanking
- thinking
- sharing
- giving
- loving
- together yet personal.

2. Why do we have assembly?

- It's the law (and that was the very first answer given by a governor's child!). So we can gather together for us to think about things and each other,
- sing songs
- learn about God
- worship
- teachers can explain
- showing and sharing
- news of clubs/events/garden
- acting stories
- announcements from outside school

3. What makes a good school? -

- ☺ caring for each other
- ☺ people working together
- ☺ discipline
- ☺ friends
- ☺ children being good, e.g. try hard, learn and think, quiet in assembly and lessons
- ☺ teachers, cooks, dinner ladies, secretary, caretaker all work together
- ☺ pets
- ☺ noiseless heaters (ours never were!)
- ☺ nice dinners
- ☺ pleasant surroundings/good 'atmosphere' or feeling
- ☺ uniform was mentioned by one child but only after the children consulted their parents!

4. 'The simple things of life'—

- a laugh
- teddy-bear
- sweets
- skipping rope
- music
- cornflakes
- cosy in bed
- marbles
- dressing up
- talk with a friend
- colours
- lolly sticks
- hot bath
- conkers
- good book
- bread
- a lesson learnt
- pencils

5. 'Christmas time is . . .'

- a warm feeling inside that tells you to get up early
- cards to send
- angels singing
- decorating the tree
- happiness with all the family
- tiring!
- magic
- the celebration of Jesus' birth
- peace and candles glowing
- spending money on others
- giving and sharing
- excitement and surprises

This, of necessity, is just a selection of ideas offered.

Someone Special

Appendix D

Conflict Resolution Rap

Conflict resolution is where it's at.
So listen as we begin to rap:

You are you and I am me,
But we are us, and us are we!

Identify the problem, bring it out.
Don't kick or punch, or even shout.
Attack the problem and not the fear.
Listen with an open mind and ear.

'Cause
You are you and I am me,
But we are us, and us are we!

Focus on the problem, don't leave it behind.
Treat others with respect and feelings kind.
Take responsibility for your action,
And you'll get a feeling of satisfaction.

'Cause
You are you and I am me,
But we are us, and us are we!

Not listening to others is really unhip,
So listen to me, I'll give you a tip,
No bossing, no threatening, no put-down names.
No making excuses, no passing the blame.

'Cause
You are you and I am me,
But we are us, and us are we!

Bringing up the past is not very cool.
So whoever does, is really a fool,
And getting even is really unkind.
Don't use your hands, only your mind!

'Cause
You are you and I am me,
But we are us, and us are we!

(Used with permission. © Schmidt and Friedman, 'Peaceworks', from *Fighting Fair – Martin Luther King Jnr. for Kids*.)

Appendix E

AND GOD SAID . . .

And God said . . .
'Let there be light in my new world
Where night gives way to each new day.'
And God looked at the light that He had made
And He saw that it was good.

And God said . . .
'Let there be space in my new world
A sky of blue, the deep sea too.'
And God looked at the space that He had made
And He saw that it was good.

And God said . . .
'Let there be plants in my new world
With flowers and leaves and fruits and seeds.'
And God looked at the plants that He had made
And He saw that they were good.

And God said . . .
'Let there be stars in my new world
The sunshine bright the moon by night.'
And God looked at the stars that He had made
And He saw that they were good.

And God said . . .
'Let there be creatures in my new world
To run, swim, fly and multiply.'
And God looked at the creatures He had made
And He saw that they were good.

And God said . . .
'Let there be people in my new world,
I'd like to share my world so fair.'
And God said the people living there,
'Now it's your world too, so please take care
Of all living kinds both great and small
I love them all.'

© **Pamela Dew**

And God said...

Pamela Dew

[Musical score]

1. And God said... 'Let there be light in my new world, where night gives way to each new day.' And God looked at the light that He had made, and He saw that it was good.

Last time to Coda

CODA

living there, 'Now it's your world too, so please take care of all living kinds, both great and small, I love them all.'

Copyright © 1997
International copyright secured. All rights reserved. Used by permission.

Appendix F

Overhead transparencies

1. Money, Money, Money (© Susan Dew)
2. Choices *(Assembly 2)* (© Susan Dew)
3. Unto us a child is born (© Deaconess P Willetts)
4. Co-operation (© Susan Dew)
5. I walked 5 steps today (© Shaftesbury Society)
6. Faces *(Assembly 5)* (© Tear Fund)
7. Football fans
8. Animals on the march
9. A boy in Africa eats (© Tear Fund)
10. Patterns (© Biblical Creation Society)
11. Shanty town in Zaire (© Tear Fund)
12. Kurdish refugees (© Tear Fund)
13. The road to school (© Unicef)
14. Two harvest success stories (© Tearfund)
15. Osprey *(Assembly 12)* (© Natural History Picture Agency)

Two Innovative Religious Education Resource Books

Postbag from Palestine

and

Mailbag from the Middle East

by

DIANE WALKER

illustrated by Jane Taylor

Postbag from Palestine and *Mailbag from the Middle East* are practical aids for primary school teachers each containing:

- lively re-tellings of well-known Bible stories from the Old and New Testaments
- a full colour illustration for each story
- significant photocopiable elements
- activity suggestions encouraging exploration of the stories
- questions to stimulate conversation
- reflections
- 17 scripted assemblies
- an innovative postbag

In *Postbag from Palestine* and *Mailbag from the Middle East*, the subject of each chapter is introduced in the form of postcards, diary entries, letters and faxes from key figures in the stories. The questions, activities and follow-up ideas offer a range of stimuli to engage children's interest and to promote the teaching of RE and history in a lively, pro-active way.

Diane Walker has taught English and RE at secondary level, and has also taught in primary schools. She is the co-author of a series of three books on the use of the Bible in primary schools and has adapted Bible stories for this age group.

Jane Taylor is a professional artist whose field of interest is educational and narrative illustration. She has worked on projects for the Association of Christian Teachers, the Bible Society and Eagle, amongst others.

Postbag from Palestine: 0 86347 142 0
Mailbag from the Middle East: 0 86347 199 4

FAITH IN HISTORY

Ideas for RE, History and Assembly
in the Primary School

by

Margaret Cooling

Faith in History is:
- Based on the history of Christianity
- For use with 7 to 12 year-olds
- Designed to encourage pupils to learn from the past
- Lavishly illustrated throughout

Faith in History covers:
- Romans, Saxons and Vikings
- Tudors and Stuarts
- Victorian Britain
- Britain since 1930
- Churches throughout the ages

Faith in History contains:
- 54 different topics
- Background information for teachers
- Primary and secondary source material
- Practical activities for pupils
- Photocopiable elements
- An introduction examining important educational issues

Worksheets to accompany *Faith in History* are also available separately. Presented in four thematic packs – *Invaders and Settlers; Tudors & Stuarts; Victorian Britain* and *Britain Post 1930* – or one pack containing all four sets. the worksheets are fully photocopiable, are printed on durable card, contain a variety of activities and are suitable for individual, group or class work.

Margaret Cooling is the author of a number of books on primary school religious education and assemblies and regularly leads INSET courses for teachers. She is employed by the Association of Christian Teachers and is based at Stapleford House Education Centre, Nottingham.

Faith in History (book) 0 86347 106 4
Faith in History worksheets -
    complete set 0 86347 133 1
    Invaders & settlers 0 86347 134 X
    Tudors & Stuarts 0 86347 135 8
    Victorian Britain 0 86347 136 6
    Britain post 1930 0 86347 137 4

Unto us a child is born

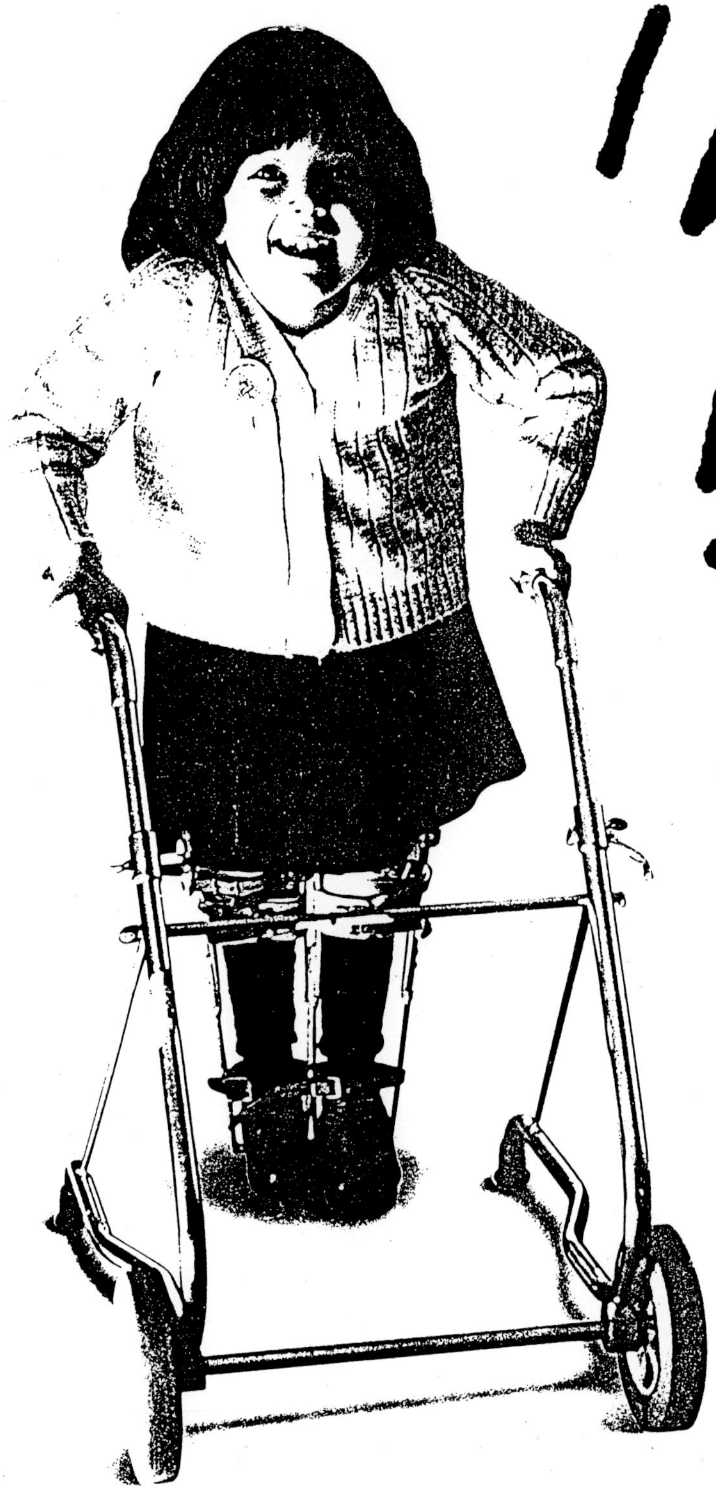

I walked
5 steps
today

Shaftesbury

150 years of Christian care in action

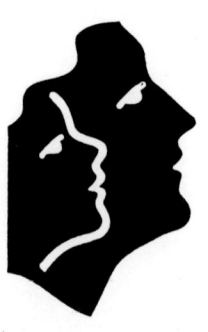

5

Ahmed (Kabul, Afghanistan - photo: Zeba Media)